THREE SEXUAL REVOLUTIONS

Catholic ~ Protestant ~ Atheist

A Sociological & Historical Perspective

David R. Carlin

lectio
Lectio Publishing, LLC
Hobe Sound, Florida, USA

www.lectiopublishing.com

Cover and Book Design: Linda Wolf

Paperback ISBN 978-1-943901-21-0
Library of Congress Control Number: 2021953550
e-Book ISBN 978-1-943901-23-4

Published by Lectio Publishing, LLC
Hobe Sound, Florida 33455
www.lectiopublishing.com

Dedication

To my three children:
David III, Joshua, Margaret.

CONTENTS

PART III

EPILOGUE

Acknowledgments

Thanks to my wife Maureen,
without whose support and encouragement
this book would not have been possible.

Introduction

The great American sexual revolution commenced in the 1960s. Still going on today, its latest demand is that we should all recognize and endorse the exceedingly weird phenomenon called transgenderism; we should believe, that is to say, that a man/boy is a woman/girl if he feels that he is, and that a woman/girl is a man/boy if she feels that she is. Earlier in its career the sexual revolution demanded that we approve of fornication, unmarried sexual cohabitation, out-of-wedlock childbirth, pornography, no-fault divorce, abortion, homosexuality, and same-sex marriage. The revolution has been relatively successful in its previous demands, which have been complied with not simply by huge sections of the general public but also by the US Supreme Court; and as a result the USA is, morally speaking, a very different country from what it was prior to the 1960s. Those on the cultural left will tell us that the USA is a much better country thanks to this sexual revolution; those on the cultural right (among whom is the author of this book) will tell us that the USA is much worse than it might have been.

But this is not the first sexual revolution in human history. There have been many, both big revolutions and smaller revolutions. In this book I will discuss three of the big revolutions: (1) the Catholic revolution, (2) the Protestant revolution, and (3) the atheistic revolution—this last being the name which, it seems to me, can with justice be assigned to the current revolution.

Let me note in passing that I am writing this book, not as a philosopher or theologian, but as a sociologist and historian.

Part I

The Catholic Sexual Revolution

When Christianity entered the Roman Empire it brought with it a code of sexual morality that was radically different from the sexual permissiveness that prevailed in the Roman world—a degree of permissiveness that may have been equal to, or nearly equal to, the permissiveness that prevails in modern America. However, the student of history needs to be cautious here. While we know a vast amount about the degree of sexual permissiveness in modern America, and while we know a pretty good amount about the degree of sexual permissiveness in upper-class Rome in the first centuries BC and AD, we don't know very much about the degree of permissiveness among the Roman middle and lower classes. We have to make an educated guess.

My own guess is that the middle and lower classes were divided in their attitudes toward sexual conduct. Many, mimicking the behavior of their social betters, were permissive; upper-class sexual morality (or rather immorality) "trickled down" to them. Many others, reacting with disgust at the sexual immorality of the higher classes, felt a nostalgic attachment to the legendary strict sexual morals of early Rome. This latter group would later be ripe for conversion to Christianity, a religion that offered—or rather, demanded—a strict sexual morality.

1

Roman Sexual Morality

Early Rome—I mean Rome of the kings and the early republic—greatly prized female chastity and honored the men who respected the chastity of wives and maidens. At least it was so according to legend; according, that is, to the stories Romans told themselves about their early history. For instance, when, about the year 500 BC, Lucretia, the chaste young wife of a Roman patrician, was raped by young Tarquin, the son of the King of Rome, so ashamed was she that her chastity had been violated that she committed suicide—but only after revealing what had happened to her husband and his friends, and only after having them swear that they would avenge Tarquin's crime and her disgrace. Only when they had made this promise did she plunge a sword into her formerly chaste breast. As a result, Tarquin, the last king, was expelled from the city and Rome became a republic (about 505 BC).

For centuries Roman women were as famous for their chastity as Roman men were for their courage. But toward the latter days of the republic, things had changed considerably—at least on the chastity front.

An anecdote from the first century BC illustrates the tone of Roman sexual morality about a century prior to the coming of Christianity, a story that has to do with three persons: Julius Caesar, his wife, and his wife's adulterous lover, a man named Publius Clodius. In the days before he became the sole ruler (or perpetual dictator—his official title) of the Empire, when he was still no more than an ambitious and high-ranking politician, Julius Caesar happened to hold an important priestly office (even though Caesar may have been an atheist). He was the Pontifex Maximus, the high priest of the city.[1] At some point during the year the wife of the Pontifex Maximus had the duty of presiding over a religious rite honoring the so-called Good Goddess (Bona Dea). This ritual, which was conducted by women, and women alone, took twenty-four hours to complete, and it was held in the home of the Pontifex and his wife. During the ceremony only women were allowed in the house; no men were allowed, not even the Pontifex himself.

Now it so happened that Mrs. Caesar was at the time conducting an adulterous affair with Publius Clodius, another ambitious Roman politician who just happened to be a political associate of Caesar. Caesar, it seems, had no objection to his wife's affair (he himself engaged in adulteries, and he was sufficiently fair-minded not to demand that his wife behave better than he did)—provided the affair was carried on with discretion, causing no public scandal. Besides, the political party supporting Caesar also supported Clodius. Tolerating his wife's affair was a way for Caesar to strengthen his political alliances.

Clodius figured that the ceremony of the Good Goddess, when Caesar would be out of the house for twenty-four hours, would be a fine opportunity to spend the night with Mrs. Caesar. But there was a problem: only women were allowed in the house during the ceremony. And so Clodius, in order to carry out his plan, dressed himself in women's clothing, and in this disguise he entered the house, where he remained overnight. Unfortunately for all concerned, some of the women in the house spotted him, and within a few days the report was all over Rome that Clodius had spent the night in Caesar's bed with Caesar's wife.

Well, while Caesar didn't mind his wife's adultery provided she did it discreetly, social convention required that Caesar divorce his wife once the adultery became publicly known. And so he did. But convention also required that he sue Clodius for the offense. But he didn't do this. After all, Clodius was a political ally; why antagonize him by suing him? People challenged Caesar, asking

[1] It was a title that the popes later claimed for themselves when they, though representing a new religion, were also the high priests of the city of Rome. And so today's pope is the successor not just of St. Peter, but also of Julius Caesar.

why he would divorce his wife for adultery while taking no action against Clodius for the very same offense. Now Caesar couldn't very well speak candidly, saying that both his action against his wife and his inaction against Clodius were motivated by purely political considerations. So Caesar (a clever man if ever there was one) said that he only *suspected* Clodius of adultery; he wasn't sure; and suspicion was not a sufficient basis for suing a man. Likewise he only suspected his wife. But in the case of his wife suspicion was enough to justify action, for "Caesar's wife must be above suspicion."

Another Roman story, from a half-century or so later, further illustrates the tone of upper-class Roman sexual morality. The Emperor Augustus (this was Octavian, the great-nephew of Julius Caesar whom Caesar in his will had adopted as his son) had been none too virtuous in his ruthless climb to power. For instance, in order to make an alliance with Mark Antony, he gave the green light to Antony's assassination of Cicero, even though Cicero, who despised Antony, had been an early and indispensable supporter of Octavian. Again, Octavian chose Livia as his wife even though Livia was already married to Octavian's friend Tiberius Nero, and even though Livia, at the time of her wedding to Octavian, was pregnant with a child by her first husband. Livia was Octavian's third and final wife, apparently the only woman he ever truly loved. She and Augustus never had any children of their own. She was the mother, by Tiberius Nero, of Tiberius, who would become, thanks to his mother's efforts (some of them criminal), Augustus's successor as Roman Emperor. (It would be during the reign of Tiberius that the crucifixion of Jesus would take place at Jerusalem, located at the eastern end of the Empire.)

In any case, once securely in power as the sole ruler of the Empire, Augustus became a moral conservative. He wanted to restore the level of virtue that had, according to legend, marked the early Republic, including especially the level of chastity that had been typical of early Roman women. Among the moral reforms of Augustus was a law that made adultery (female adultery, that is) a criminal offense. Soon after enactment of this law, however, Augustus discovered that one of the great violators of the law was his own daughter Julia, who, though married (married in fact to her step-brother, the future emperor Tiberius), had the bad habit of going to bed with men who were not her husband. Augustus was enraged, and he punished his daughter by confining her to an island upon which no man was allowed to set foot.

Another story or two. It was widely believed that Clodius, the above-mentioned lover of Mrs. Caesar, was also the incestuous lover of his own sister. Cicero, a great political foe of Clodius, often alluded to this rumor in his speeches. Cicero was also a great political foe of Mark Antony, and in his denunciations of Antony he did not hesitate to remind his listeners of the rumor that Antony when a teenage boy had been the boyfriend of a pederastic lover. Now the fact that prominent men may have been engaged in incestuous and pederastic relationships tells us something about the sexual permissiveness of Rome in the first century BC. But the fact that Cicero could use these relationships as a way to blacken the reputation of his political enemies also tells us something—that incest and pederasty, though practiced, were far from universally approved.

Bad as Roman sexual corruptions were in the age of Caesar and Augustus, they were perhaps even worse a generation or two later, at least if we may judge by the lives of some of the first century AD emperors, which we may read about in the brief biographies written by Suetonius (who lived in the late first and early second centuries AD).[2] Here are some examples, the first three drawn from the words of Suetonius:

- Of Tiberius (p. 131): "Some aspects of his criminal obscenity are almost too vile to discuss, much less believe. Imagine training little boys, whom he called his 'minnows,' to chase him while he went swimming and get between his legs to lick and nibble him."
- Of Caligula (p. 167): "He had not the slightest regard for chastity . . . and was accused of homosexual relations, both active and passive . . . Besides incest with his sisters, and a

[2] Suetonius, *The Twelve Caesars*, translated by Robert Graves (Penguin Classics, 1957).

notorious passion for prostitute Pyrallis, he made advances to almost every well-known married woman in Rome."

- Of Nero (p. 223): "Not satisfied with seducing free-born boys and married women, Nero raped the Vestal Virgin Rubria. . . . Having tried to turn the boy Sporus into a girl by castration, he went through a wedding ceremony with him – dowry, bridal veil, and all—which the whole court attended; and then brought him home, and treated him as a wife."
- The sexual improprieties of the Emperor Claudius were relatively tame. He married four times. He divorced his first two wives, and had his third executed. His fourth wife was his niece, a marriage Romans considered to be incestuous. Whatever shortcomings in sexual immorality may have marked the career of Claudius, these were more than made up for by his third wife, Messalina, a notorious adulteress. It was rumored that, while empress, she once won a competition with a prostitute to see which of them could have sex with more men in a 24-hour period; and that, again while empress, she sometimes volunteered as a prostitute in a brothel. When Claudius became convinced that she and one of her lovers were plotting to de-throne him, he had her put to death.[3]

And so the scene is set. A sexually strict religion, Christianity, enters the sexually permissive Roman Empire. It would have been easy to foresee that the new religion would be welcomed by some (sexual conservatives) with open arms and by others (sexual libertarians) with scorn and hatred.

[3] For these stories see the entry for Messalina in Wikipedia.

2

Romans and the Jewish Religion

Prior to the emergence of Christianity, the Roman Empire stretched from the Atlantic in the west to the Euphrates in the east, and from the Sahara in the south to what would later be called Scotland in the north. Many inhabitants of this vast expanse, both citizens and non-citizens alike, had developed a great interest in the religion of the Jewish people. Jews were to be found in the Empire not just in their homeland of Palestine but also in many of the big cities of the Empire, especially Alexandria (Egypt) and Rome itself.

For example, the Apostle Paul was from a middle-sized city outside of Palestine, Tarsus, located in what today is Turkey. Hence non-Jewish people in the Empire had plenty of opportunity to become acquainted with Jews and their strange religion—strange, that is, by Greco-Roman standards.

Many of those people found this "strange" religion very attractive. Yet not many of these people, who were known to the Jews as "God-fearers," actually became full-fledged converts. They stood at the door without fully entering. They became in effect semi-Jews. What attracted them to the Jewish religion? Two things especially, its monotheism and its sexual ethic.

(1) Monotheism. By the age of Caesar (first century BC) the polytheism that had dominated the Greco-Roman world from time immemorial had largely lost its plausibility. It was a religion that had been socially based on the system of city-states that had dominated Greece and Italy for many centuries. But now these old city-states had lost much of their significance, swallowed up as they were in the great Roman Empire. If the social basis of the

belief in a multitude of gods had collapsed, how could belief in the many gods survive? Further, if the Empire has a single head, the emperor, how odd it would be if the universe were governed by a multitude of gods, often a squabbling multitude. If there is only one emperor, isn't it likely that there is only one God?

There were three reactions to this fading away of the pagan gods.

(a) Atheism. If the traditional gods didn't exist, there could be no divine power. The great literary example of this atheism was the long Latin poem written by Lucretius, an Epicurean poet-philosopher, *De Rerum Naturam* (*On the Nature of Things*), which expounded the Epicurean system of belief. Julius Caesar himself, a contemporary of Lucretius, may well have been an atheist—even though he once held Rome's highest priestly office, that of Pontifex Maximus.

(b) A purely ritualistic, non-dogmatic religion. Priests and priestesses would perform traditional religious rituals, and ordinary persons would participate in these rituals, but nobody—neither the priestly performers nor the lay participants—was expected to believe the traditional stories about the gods that explained and justified these rituals.

(c) A vague belief in gods. You might reject all traditional beliefs about the gods, the beliefs for example contained in conventional mythology, but even though you rejected *those* gods you stopped short of atheism. You continued to believe that there were *some* gods, or at least some divine higher powers, even though you had no specific information about them.

(d) Polytheism as disguised monotheism. You believed that there is one God only, not many gods. But you also held that belief in the many gods is really a belief in the many aspects of the one God. For instance, belief in Zeus (Jupiter) was belief in the power of God; belief in Apollo was belief in the wisdom of God; and so on. So you could participate in rituals honoring this or that god while believing that you are honoring the one true God.

(e) Eastern gods. For a few centuries now, ever since the time of Alexander the Great (fourth century BC), eastern religions and eastern gods (that is, religions and gods from Egypt, Syria, Persia, etc.) had been filtering into the Greco-Roman world. Many, rejecting the Greek and Roman gods entirely, turned to these foreign gods.

(f) The Jewish religion. Judaism was one of these eastern religions, but it was the most unequivocal in its monotheism. It held that there is one God, and one God only, and that any kind of polytheism was to be quite definitely condemned. If you were a Greek or Roman looking for monotheism, you found it in its purest form among the Jews.

(2) Sexual ethic. If you did not like the ethic of sexual permissiveness that prevailed in Rome, at least among the higher social classes and probably among much of the rest of the population as well, and if you considered this sexual immorality not only indecent in itself but a very sad thing in comparison with the chastity of early Rome—if so, you would find very attractive the chastity demanded by the Jewish religion. One of the great commandments issued by the Jewish God was, "Thou shalt not commit adultery." And this commandment applied to men as well as women. This was a level of chastity that surpassed even the chastity of early Rome, where women were exceedingly chaste while men were granted a certain amount of license. More, among the Jews chastity was expected even among unmarried persons, and not just among unmarried females. All Jews were expected to marry and to use their sexual capacities for the production of children. If you were a Roman disgusted with the sexual immorality prevalent in the Empire, Judaism gave you just what you wanted.

Though many gentiles found Judaism to be attractive, not many, as noted above, became fully converted to the Jewish religion. Instead they were semi-converts. What prevented them from going all the way? Two things.

First, if they were to become full-fledged Jews they would be required (if male) to undergo circumcision. This rite was normally imposed on Jewish boys soon after birth. It was one thing to require this of infant boys; it was something else to require it of adult males. No doubt this requirement discouraged many gentiles from making a full conversion to a religion they admired.

Second, if they were to become full-fledged Jews, these gentiles would be expected to observe, not just the famous Ten Commandments, to which they would have no objection, but another six-hundred-plus commandments, most of these being more ritualistic than of a moral nature.

But if they stopped short of becoming full Jews, they could become semi-Jews; they could still have the benefits of Jewish monotheism and Jewish morality, especially sexual morality. Small wonder, then, that some historians estimate that on the eve of the appearance of Christianity these semi-Jewish "God-fearers" may have made up between ten and fifteen percent of the population of the Empire.

3

Gradual Conversion of Rome to Christianity

The first wave of converts to Christianity was made up of Jews in Palestine. The second and far more numerous wave was outside Palestine, among the God-fearers. They found Christianity attractive, even more attractive than Judaism, for a number of reasons. What were some of these reasons?

- Christianity had the great advantages of Judaism (monotheism, strict sexual ethic) along with none of the disadvantages (circumcision, 600-plus commandments).
- With regard to the Jewish religion, the God-fearers were, so to speak, second-class citizens. In Christianity they were first-class members.
- Christianity offered Jesus, the God-man. Judaism did not.
- While the Jewish religion offered (except for the sect of the Sadducees) the promise of everlasting life in Heaven for good persons, Christianity not only offered the same but it gave a concrete example of somebody, Jesus, who had demonstrated by his Resurrection that life after death is possible.

The third and most numerous wave of converts to Christianity was made up of gentiles who were neither Jews nor God-fearers. By the second half of the first century AD, Christianity, which at first had seemed to be no more than a sect of Judaism,[1] had become a religion distinct from the Jewish religion. It was becoming a Roman religion, moving slowly but surely in the direction of becoming the dominant religion in the Empire, although it would

[1] First-century Judaism had numerous sects: Pharisees, Sadducees, Essenes, Zealots.

not achieve that status until early in the 300s, during the reign of Constantine the Great.

When Christianity entered the Empire and began to expand, it brought with it a code of morality that banned—for members of the Church only, since for centuries the Church did not have the power to impose these bans on anybody other than Christians—the following practices, all of which were common in Roman society:

- premarital sex
- adultery
- homosexuality
- pornography
- abortion
- infanticide

And so Christianity, as it gradually came to prevail in the Empire, brought with it a great sexual revolution—not a pro-freedom revolution (like the sexual revolution of the twentieth century), but a pro-restraint revolution, a pro-chastity revolution.

The pre-Christian Greco-Roman world had a recognized list of moral virtues. *First of all*, the four cardinal virtues recognized by a wide range of philosophers: wisdom, justice, courage, and moderation.

- Moral wisdom (or to give it its Latin name, *prudentia*), or good judgment, is the virtue that enables us to judge rightly when faced with a moral question.
- Justice is the virtue that enables us to treat other persons with fairness, showing respect for their rights.
- Courage is the virtue that enables us to endure pains and hardships that may fall upon us as we attempt to live our lives in a morally correct manner.
- Moderation (or temperance) is the virtue that enables us to limit and keep under control our pursuit of pleasure, especially sensual pleasures.

Second, some widely recognized virtues that happened not to be on the standard list of cardinal virtues.

- Love of friends. Not universal love, not love of the entire human race; but love for a small number of particular persons.

- Patriotism or love of one's city-state or country.
- Clemency. An attitude that enables us to overlook injuries that have been done to us. This was especially recommended by the first century AD Stoic philosopher Seneca. And it was (rather unwisely) practiced by Julius Caesar when he pardoned many of the Romans who had opposed him in the Civil War, including men who would later assassinate him on the Ides of March, 44 BC.

Third, some lesser virtues that applied, not to everyone, but to certain socially inferior classes of people.

- Chastity. This was a virtue women were supposed to have—even though, to judge from the above stories about Caesar's wife and the daughter of Augustus, it is likely that many upper-class Roman women on the eve of the coming of Christianity didn't take the trouble to practice this virtue. All the same, it was a still-recognized ideal, and you could blacken a woman's reputation by showing that she did not live up to it. The ideal was that a woman would remain a virgin until marriage and would be sexually faithful during marriage. This virtue of chastity, however, did not apply to men. While a good man was expected to be moderate in his sexual desires and to abstain from sexual relations with the wives of other men (at least the wives of men of his own social class), he was not expected to be the least bit virginal in his premarital days; nor was he expected to strictly abstain, even in marriage, from sexual relations with slaves, whether male or female.
- Humility. This was a virtue of slaves. A good slave was a humble slave. That is to say, good slaves recognized that they occupied a lowly place in society, and they accepted this. They didn't rebel against their condition. They didn't get "uppity." Of course some slaves were uppity; they had the feeling that they were as good as their masters. But insofar as they had this feeling they were not good slaves; they lacked the virtue of humility. Needless to say, this was not a virtue for free persons. Those in the higher classes were expected to be proud, very proud. Even those in the lower classes of free

persons were expected to have some pride, for at least they were socially superior to slaves.

Then, beginning in the first century AD, came the great Christian moral revolution. The new religion retained, while modifying and intensifying, the pagan virtues. Let's look at how Christianity transformed these pre-Christian virtues. The morality of natural law, while retained, was supplemented and improved by a morality of supernatural law; that is, a moral law based on Divine Revelation.

- **Wisdom**. Good moral judgment, in addition to being based on natural law, tradition, and personal experience, must also be based on Christian wisdom, a divinely revealed wisdom that had not been available to pre-Christian pagans.
- **Justice**. If justice is defined as "giving every person his or her due" (a traditional definition), the Christian teaching that every person is equal in the eyes of God implied that the average person was due much more respect than pagans had believed.
- **Courage**. The courage of the pagans was an active courage, the courage needed to confront and do battle against enemies; the courage, for example, of the soldier in warfare. Christian courage was a more passive kind of courage, a willingness to suffer and even die for the truth; the courage exemplified by Jesus on the cross and by many Christian martyrs.
- **Moderation**. Good pagans would avoid excess in their pursuit of pleasure. Good Christians would go beyond this; they would embrace ascetic mortification of the flesh.
- **Friendship**. Christianity taught that we should be prepared to extend friendship not just to a small group of particular persons, but to everybody, even strangers, even enemies. (See Jesus' parable of the Good Samaritan.)
- **Patriotism**. The object of Christian patriotism was not the temporal commonwealth (the Roman state) but the spiritual commonwealth (the Christian Church). Just as the Roman patriot would devote his life to Rome and be willing if need be to die for Rome, so the Christian patriot would devote his life to the Church and be willing to die if need be for the

Church. And this spiritual commonwealth included not just Roman Christians but all Christians, no matter what country they might live in; and not just living Christians but saintly Christians who had moved on to the heavenly afterlife.

- **Clemency**. Christians were expected, not just to overlook the sins committed against them by their enemies (Julius Caesar was willing to do that), but to go one great step further; they were expected to love their enemies.
- **Chastity**. In Christianity this feminine virtue was elevated to the status of a universal virtue. Sexual standards were equalized between men and women. Males too were expected to live according to traditional feminine standards of sexual virtue. In the sexual revolution that took place in the USA beginning in the 1960s, sexual standards were also equalized between men and women; but in the modern case this meant that women were now free to behave in accordance with the traditional (and relatively "loose") sexual standards that applied to men. The two sexual revolutions—the ancient Christian one and the modern secular one—were precisely the opposite of one another.
- **Humility**. Just as chastity, a feminine virtue, was universalized by Christianity, so humility, a servile virtue, was universalized so as to apply to everybody, even persons of great wealth and power; even kings and emperors. If in the Incarnation God humbled himself to become a lowly human, why shouldn't kings adopt a slave-like humility in the face of God?

4

Christian Hyper-chastity

What inspired the early Christians to attach themselves to the virtue of chastity? Or let us call it the virtue of *hyper-chastity*, for Christian chastity was a degree of chastity that went beyond anything the ancient pre-Christian world had imagined, and goes far beyond any degree of sexual restraint the present-day world approves. From the point of view of the Roman secular world, early Christian chastity was much too strict. And from the point of view of today's secular world, early Christian chastity was ludicrous if not perverse. It was a degree of chastity that banned many sexual practices along with certain practices closely connected with sex. The following were banned by early Christianity:

- premarital sex (fornication)
- pornography
- unchaste thoughts and feelings
- adultery
- polygamy
- homosexual practice
- divorce and remarriage
- contraception[1]
- abortion
- infanticide

But why? Why did early Christianity have such a strict attitude, an attitude that did not tolerate even a small amount of sexual

[1] I am not aware of any documentary evidence from the days of early Christianity showing that the Church banned marital contraception; but, given the general Christian attitude toward sex, I think it is a reasonable inference that the Church disapproved of contraception.

laxity? Why was it so radically different from the ancient world's rather permissive attitude toward sex by males and even more radically different from *today's* highly permissive attitude toward sex by both males and females?

To answer these questions, we should notice the following factors found in the Gospels.

- Above all, the example of Jesus. It seems clear that he was unmarried; and given that he was a good Jew (let alone that he was divine), we may assume that he did not engage in non-marital sexual activity. (I say this with all due respect to Dan Brown, author of *The DaVinci Code*, and all other silly moderns who like to imagine, preposterously, that Jesus and Mary Magdalene were either married to one another or, worse still, were unmarried lovers.)
- The statement of Jesus that there is no marriage in Heaven. (See Mark 12:25 and corresponding passages in Matthew and Luke). If Heaven is a place of holiness, the very highest level of holiness, and if marriage and sex are not found in Heaven, then it seems to follow that abstention from marriage and sex is favorable to achieving holiness even here on Earth. Chaste celibacy is a kind of first step toward heavenly holiness.
- Jesus said that the man who looks at a woman with lust has committed adultery in his heart. (Matthew 5:27-28) Presumably he would say the same about a woman who looks at a man with lust. Chastity of conduct is not enough; one must also be chaste in thought and feeling.
- Jesus said that divorce-and-remarriage, though allowed by the law of Moses because of the hardness of human hearts (or perhaps Jewish hearts), is not allowed by the law of God. It was not that way in the beginning. Jesus said, "What therefore God hath joined together, let no man put asunder." (Mark 10:9)
- Jesus said that whoever remarries after divorce commits adultery.[2] (Luke 16:18)

---

[2] Beginning with Luther, even the strictest Protestantism has allowed divorce for adultery, appealing to the Gospel of Matthew, which, in contrast to the Gospels of Mark and Luke, has Jesus allowing divorce for "porneia"—one possible translation of which is "adultery." Given that the other two Synoptics

- Jesus said that some persons are "eunuchs" for the sake of Heaven—quickly adding that not everybody is called to this state. It is reasonable to assume that when he spoke of eunuchs he was not speaking literally but metaphorically; that is, he was not speaking of men who had been castrated, but was speaking of men (and women) who had chosen a life of celibacy for the sake of Heaven.
- In the gospels of Matthew and Luke, we are told that Mary, the mother of Jesus, became miraculously pregnant by the power of the Holy Ghost while remaining a virgin.
- Though it is not mentioned in any of the gospels, it soon became a common Christian belief that Mary, though married to Joseph, remained a lifelong virgin.
- St. Paul had a strongly pro-chastity attitude, an attitude exhibited at many points in his epistles, but nowhere more clearly than in First Corinthians (7:8-9): "To the unmarried and the widows I say that it is well for them to remain unmarried as I am. But if they are not practicing self-control, they should marry. For it is better to marry than to be aflame with passion."[3]

And how did the early Church respond to all this? For one thing, it repudiated the sexual freedom typical of the pre-Christian ancient world by promulgating the bans (from fornication to infanticide) listed above. Second, it held virgins in great honor, along with widows who abstained from remarriage. Third, beginning in the third century, it held in even greater honor monks and nuns

do not mention this exception, and given the anti-divorce attitudes of the early Church, it is probable that "adultery" is not the best translation of "porneia." It is more likely that "porneia" in this context refers to an immoral cohabitation relationship; a fornication relationship. Jesus is probably saying that a man cannot end a married relationship with a woman, but he may end a cohabitation relationship—as, for example, St. Augustine later did. See a further discussion of this topic below, Chapter 9, "Freedom to Divorce and Remarry."

[3] This is from the New Revised Standard Version. The King James Version of this famous passage reads as follows: "I say therefore to the unmarried and widows, It is good for them if they abide even as I. But if they cannot contain, let them marry: for it is better to marry than to burn." The Douay-Rheims Version (the Catholic translation of the same era as the KJV) is almost exactly the same; its final sentence reads: "For it is better to marry than to burn."

who lived lives of asceticism, an asceticism that notably included chaste celibacy.

There was more to monastic asceticism than lifelong abstention from sex and marriage. Among other things there were fasts and sparse diets and rough clothing and hard beds to sleep on; and plenty of hard work. And there was more to monasticism than asceticism: there was, for example, an endless round of prayer. Of course, in the long history of monasticism there were monks and nuns who fell short of the ideal, and there were even more than a few who fell short of the chastity portion of that ideal. Who can be surprised at that, human nature being weak, even in those with an apparent vocation to holiness of life? Besides, over the centuries many men and women entered monasteries and convents without having genuine vocations; they were pushed into the monastic life by family pressures or other social circumstances.

All the same, the monastic ideal persisted in the Catholic world for many centuries, no matter how often individuals and entire monasteries fell short of the ideal. And the ideal was attractive, not just to those Catholics who felt "called" to the monastic life, but to the vast majority of ordinary Catholics, men and women who themselves had no wish to live ascetic lives (although the harsh social and economic circumstances of their times often forced them to live uncomfortable lives of involuntary poverty even outside of monasteries) or to abstain from sex (one of the few pleasures in life available to chronically poor people). Ordinary Christian men and women did not themselves wish to be monks or nuns, but they thought of monks and nuns as morally and religiously "superior" people; their state in life was a "higher" state; they were thought of as being closer to God, closer to Heaven. By admiring them, by showing them due respect, and by supporting them with material goods, it was felt that ordinary Catholics themselves came closer to Heaven. If these laypersons were not hyper-chaste themselves, they were, it may be said, *vicariously* hyper-chaste by virtue of their great admiration and respect for monks and nuns. If the Church on Earth was like an army (the "Church militant"), monks and nuns were the combat troops of the army; everybody else, the great majority of Catholics, were either useful support troops or camp followers. The victories of our monks and nuns were our victories; all Catholics could be proud of their fighting men and women.

As a result of many centuries of this kind of thing, the idea of chastity was inseparable from the idea of Catholicism. Catholics—even those who were great sexual sinners—were psychologically incapable of thinking that unchastity was okay in the eyes of God.

Was Jesus himself an ascetic? Yes and no. He abstained from marriage and sex, and he lived a life of considerable hardship, traveling about Palestine on foot and having no permanent home or regular source of income. Those are ascetic traits. But it seems that he did not stint on eating and drinking. He was in this regard very unlike John the Baptist, who lived barely clothed in the hot desert and fed on locusts and wild honey. There was, however, a brief period of extreme asceticism in the life of Jesus—the forty-day period when he lived in the desert, rather like the Egyptian monks of a few centuries later (see the *Life of St. Anthony* by St. Athanasius). But once he began his public life of preaching and healing, he never returned to extreme asceticism.

Does this mean that monks and nuns, by not following the relatively non-ascetic example of Jesus, were living lives that were not in conformity with the Christian ideal? No. See Matthew 9:14-15, which says:

> Then the disciples of John came to him, saying, "Why do we and the Pharisees fast, but your disciples do not fast?' And Jesus said to them, 'Can the wedding guests mourn as long as the bridegroom is with them? The days will come, when the bridegroom is taken away from them, and then they will fast."

In other words, extreme asceticism is not appropriate as long as Jesus himself is actually in our midst. But after he is gone, after his Death and Resurrection and Ascension—that will be the time for extreme asceticism; that will be the time for monks and nuns; that will be the time to live something like John the Baptist.

Catholic parish priests were also supposed to be religiously "superior" to ordinary Catholics. No small part of this superiority was based on their celibacy. For centuries this celibacy was optional, though widely practiced and widely expected of priests; but in the eleventh century the pope made it mandatory. The idea seems to have been that priests will be holier if they are chaste and celibate; that is, if they are more like monks and nuns. At all events Catholic laypersons will feel that priests are more holy if they are chaste and celibate, and as a result priests will be shown more respect and will be better listened to when they preach the gospel and when they give moral advice and religious guidance.

In sum, hyper-chastity was greatly valued in the early Catholic world—mostly, no doubt, because it was greatly valued by Jesus himself, and this high valuation had been passed on through the centuries; but partly also because a life of voluntary celibacy and chastity is in itself an extraordinary achievement. Nowadays of course the person who chooses such an "achievement" would be thought by the secular world to be a fool. But it was not so in the old days, that is, throughout most of the history of Catholicism. Then it was thought to be a nearly superhuman accomplishment, something too much for mere human nature—something in other words that suggested that the person who successfully lived this kind of chaste and celibate life must be the recipient of special supernatural aid, a special grace of God. This person (the monk or nun or celibate parish priest) must be one of God's favorites; otherwise he or she would not have been given this supernatural aid.

Picture a spectrum of sexual moral attitudes, ranging from utterly permissive at one end to utterly restrictive at the other end. The early Christian attitude was way down toward the utterly restrictive end of the scale. Our present American attitude is way down toward the utterly permissive end.

For the early Christians sexual desire was a great challenge; an obstacle that had to be resisted and overcome on the road to holiness. To be sure, it was not positively evil. After all, it was a necessary element in the process of procreation; if it did not exist, the human race would soon die out. And so it was fitting that married couples should from time to time give in to this powerful desire and have sexual intercourse with one another. But ideal Christians, that is, saintly monks and saintly nuns and saintly parish priests (not to mention saintly bishops and archbishops and cardinals) did not give in. They resisted. They said to sexual temptation, "You may be a powerful force of nature, but you will not defeat me; on the contrary, thanks to the grace of God *I* will defeat *you*."

One of the great Fathers of the Church, St. Augustine (AD 364–430), as we learn from his *Confessions*, was well acquainted with the power of sexual desire, for he led a sexually active life from his late teens until he was well past his thirtieth birthday. Without being married, he and his girlfriend cohabited for about ten years, first in North Africa, later in Italy; and they had a son together.[4] When Augustine was given a high-ranking job at the emperor's court in Milan, his now elevated social status meant that he could now make what the world would consider to be a good marriage; and so he became engaged to a socially elite young woman. Her family would not put up with his continuing to live with his girlfriend while waiting for the wedding to take place; so he broke with the girlfriend, sending her back to Africa. But he soon found that he could not do without a woman, so strong was his felt need for sexual relations; so he took a new mistress to fill in the gap between the dismissal of his former concubine and his pending wedding.

But he was now a Christian, hence he had at least a theoretical appreciation of the value of chastity. And so he prayed: "Dear God, make me chaste; but later, not now." Soon came the famous "*Tolle, lege*" ("Take and read") incident in his garden. He picked up a little book containing St. Paul's Epistle to the Romans. Opening it at random, his eyes fell on chapter 13, verses 13-14, where he read: "Let us conduct ourselves becomingly as in the day, not in reveling and drunkenness, not in debauchery and licentiousness, not in quarreling and jealousy. But put on the Lord Jesus Christ, and make no provision for the flesh, to gratify its desires." He read this passage as a message from God directed personally to him. Instantly he renounced sex forever. There would be no

[4] Tragically, this very promising boy, named Adeodatus (Gift from God), died at the age of fourteen.

girlfriend, and no wife either. Henceforth he would live a life of chaste celibacy, first as a monk, later as a priest and bishop.

Writing some years later about the Fall of Adam and Eve, Augustine, who unlike most great theologians was personally acquainted with the power of sexual desire, held that this desire was a byproduct of the Fall. It was not found in Adam and Eve prior to their sin. It was not part of human nature as originally constituted; rather, it was a punishment for the sin of our first parents. And we their children are still being punished this way; we are still burdened with the curse of sexual desire. In Eden prior to the Fall, the conduct of Adam and Eve was guided by reason, not emotion, especially not sexual emotion. In saying this, Augustine was borrowing from the Platonic/Stoic idea of the good life, a life in which reason is always in control, never the emotions.

But after the Fall, things became disordered. Emotions such as anger and, especially, sexual lust emerged and became very powerful; they often threw off the control of reason. How unfortunate it is that a married couple, in order to comply with God's command that they "increase and multiply," should have to undergo the shameful madness of sexual passion. "Any friend of wisdom and holy joys who lives a married life," says Augustine, "would prefer to beget children without lust of this kind, if such a thing were possible." [*City of God*, Book XIV, chapter 16] Could any statement be more opposed to today's prevailing attitude regarding sexual conduct?

If Adam and Eve had remained obedient to God, if they had not committed the great sin of eating the forbidden fruit, their sexual relations with one another would have involved no passion, no shame. "And the man and his wife were both naked, and were not ashamed" (Genesis 2:25)—so it was before the Fall. But immediately after their sin they first felt sexual shame. "Then the eyes of both were opened, and they knew that they were naked; and they sewed fig leaves together and made loincloths for themselves." (Genesis 3:7) After the Fall, says Augustine, all human sex involves shame, not just the illicit sex of fornication and adultery, but even the morally allowable—indeed the morally mandatory—sex that takes place between husband and wife. That is why we cover our private parts (our "shameful parts") even in the warmest weather. That is why people, whether prostitutes and their customers or chaste husbands and wives, engage in sexual relations only in privacy.

This, however, created a great theoretical problem for Augustine. The temporary madness of sexual desire seems to be a necessary condition for sexual intercourse, and sexual intercourse is a necessary condition for procreation and the continuation of the human race. And so the question arises: in Eden prior to the Fall, when there was nothing but Stoic/Platonic rationality, no madness of sexual desire, how could Adam and Eve have had sexual relations? And without sexual intercourse how could they have produced children? Was the Fall and its curse of sexual desire needed that reproduction might take place? That didn't seem to Augustine to be a good answer. After all, God had commanded them to "increase and multiply" *prior* to their having sinned; he did not wait till after their sin to command them to become the parents of the human race.

So if they had never sinned, if therefore they had never experienced the madness of sexual passion, how could they have obeyed God's command to increase and multiply? Augustine's answer was that Adam and Eve in Eden would have been able to have passion-less sexual intercourse. Their sexual organs, so little subject to rational control in the post-Eden world, would in Eden have been as much subject to control of the will as are the arms and legs and fingers of a healthy person. Without their feeling the madness of sexual passion, their reproductive organs would have been able to perform the sexual act. Adam, in Augustine's words, would have "poured his seed into his wife's womb in tranquility of mind." [*City of God*, Book XIV, chapter 26] Is that hard to believe? Not at all if we keep two things in mind: (a) that human nature is radically different today from what it was prior to the Fall, and (b) that with God all things are possible.[5]

Though many of Augustine's views either reflected or became the official views of the Catholic Church, this one did not. Centu-

[5] For Augustine's discussion of the foregoing issues, see chapters 16 through 26 of Book XIV of his magnum opus, *The City of God*. I have been consulting the translation by R. W. Dyson, Cambridge University Press, 1998.

ries later Thomas Aquinas (1224-74), usually a devoted follower of St. Augustine, simply declared that Augustine was mistaken on this point. Strong sexual desire, according to Thomas, is not an unhappy byproduct of the Fall; it is simply a facet of human nature. However, even though the Church did not adopt Augustine's view as part of its official teaching, the fact that Augustine held this view gives us some idea of what the attitude of early Catholics must have been toward the powerful force of sexual desire.

5

Gnosticism

To better understand the hyper-chastity of Christian monks and nuns in the early centuries of the Church, we should keep in mind an attitude that was widespread among many, both Christians and non-Christians, in the Greco-Roman world during the early centuries of the Christian era, especially in the first, second, and third centuries AD. It was an attitude that held, or rather *felt*, that there is something fundamentally wrong with the material world—and hence with our bodies, which are part of the material world. This pessimistic attitude is represented to some degree by those early Christians who were hyper-chaste and prone to asceticism; but it is most clearly represented by Gnosticism, which for more than a century was a great rival of Christianity, threatening for a while to take over Christianity and turn it into a Gnostic religion.

Gnosticism came in many forms, but they all conformed to the same basic pattern of beliefs, namely these.

- God exists, and God is immaterial spirit, and is entirely good.
- The world of nature, being material, is bad.
- Therefore God, being immaterial and good, could not have created our material world.
- The world of nature must, then, have been created by an evil power, an evil god or anti-God.
- Our human bodies, being material, are evil; and so are their bodily desires for food and drink and sex.
- Marriage is sinful, for it necessarily involves the sin of sexual intercourse.
- Our souls, being spiritual or immaterial, yearn for escape

from the body and union with God, the supreme Spirit.

- While it is impossible to lead a good life on Earth, which means that it is impossible to be happy in this lifetime, the least bad human life is one in which we distance ourselves from the body and its evil desires.
- Jesus (according to Christianized versions of Gnosticism) was sent by God to teach us the way of salvation.
- The body of Jesus was unreal, only an immaterial phantom; for how could Jesus, the God-sent Teacher, have an evil material body?

Christianity, while it bore a certain resemblance to Gnosticism, differed from it in fundamental ways. Instead of teaching that the world is purely evil, Christianity taught: "For God so loved the world that he gave his only son . . . Indeed God did not send the Son into the world to condemn the world, but in order that the world might be saved through him." (John: 3:16-17)

More specifically, Christianity held that:

- God is the one and only creator.
- Therefore God created the material universe.
- And thus the material universe, being God's creation, is not evil; rather, it is good.
- The physical universe, far from being the antithesis of God, is his reflection.
- The human body is not evil; nor are its desires for food, drink, sex, etc.
- Marriage is not sinful, nor is sexual intercourse between husband and wife.
- Jesus, while perfectly good, had a real human body, fully material, and this body was not evil; and it was this material body that suffered and died and rose again.
- Jesus came to us, not simply as a Teacher (as the Gnostics held), but as a Savior, saving us through his suffering and death.

All the same, Christianity too, although in a milder way, represented a turning away from the material world, a turning instead toward a heavenly world that lies well beyond the limits of this lower world. In other words, early Christianity, like Gnosticism, tended toward world-rejection—though not nearly so much as Gnosticism. Early Christianity, though its fundamental orientation was Heaven-ward, felt it had a work to do in *this* world. And because of this it was able, as the next few centuries revealed, to create on the ruins of the old Greco-Roman civilization a new Christian civilization.

Why were the people of the Roman Empire so pessimistic, so despairing, so negative, in their feelings about the world and about human life in the world? No doubt there were many reasons, one of which is the simple fact that this material world and our lives in this material world leave a lot to be desired. We are able to imagine an ideal world—a world without any of the pains and sufferings and sins and crimes of this present world. How can we fail to notice that this temporal world is very unlike the ideal world that we can so easily imagine and dream of?

Another reason for the widespread pessimism may have been a dim sense that the Roman Empire was approaching collapse. For most of its residents, the Roman Empire would have been the world itself. Romans knew that there were barbarians to the north of the empire, and barbarians to the south, and a barbarian empire (Persia) to the east. And they had heard vague rumors of great civilizations in the far east, in China and India. As for the people of the Americas, they had of course heard nothing. Practically speaking, then, for the Roman people of the early centuries AD Rome was the entire civilized world; and the collapse of Rome, therefore, would be the collapse of civilization.

Already, in the first century AD, there were signs that this collapse was coming. The most important of these signs was that the Roman *republic* had vanished, done away with by Julius Caesar and his great-nephew and adopted son Augustus. It had been replaced by a *monarchy,* and not just a token monarchy (such as Great Britain today) but an absolute monarchy in which all legitimate power was located in the emperor. Great efforts were made to disguise this fact and to pretend that the republic had survived—for everybody felt that Republican Rome was the *genuine* Rome. It was pretended, for instance, that the ultimate ruler in the state was that old and honorable institution, the Roman

Senate. It was further pretended that the Senate derived much of its authority from the people, who had delegated their authority to the Senate; and it was further pretended that the Senate, for the sake of convenience, delegated its powers to the emperor, who was in theory nothing more than an agent of the Senate. But almost nobody was fooled. Everybody knew that the Roman people no longer had power, that the Senate was no more than an honorable figurehead, and that all real power was concentrated in the hands of a single man, the emperor.

Socially and politically sensitive people knew—or rather they *felt*—that the end was coming, and not just the end for Rome but the end for civilization itself. The collapse of civilization would be in a certain sense the end of the world. Small wonder, then, that there was a widespread feeling that there is something radically wrong with the world and that our material life is barely, if at all, worth living. The end did not actually come (in the West) until the first half of the fifth century, although the Empire came close to collapse in the disastrous third century. When Alaric and his Visigoth army conquered the city of Rome and sacked it in the year AD 410, the world was horrified. This, it was felt, and felt correctly, was the beginning of the end that people had been fearing for a few centuries.

In a cultural atmosphere of world-despair and world-negation, can it be surprising that a religion/philosophy such as Gnosticism would arise and attract great numbers of adherents? And can it be surprising that Christianity, though far less world-despairing and world-negating than Gnosticism, would be influenced by this atmosphere and lean further in the direction of asceticism than its beliefs required it to do? Is it even surprising that so great a Christian theologian as Origen of Alexandria (AD 185–253) would, while a young man, have had himself castrated, apparently taking literally the words of Jesus in praise of those who become eunuchs for the sake of the Kingdom of Heaven? (Later in life Origen said that these words should *not* be taken literally.)

The earliest monks were hermits; that is, solitary ascetics living in wilderness places. The word "monk" comes from the Greek word for "alone." St. Anthony of Egypt (AD 251–356) is reputed to have been the first of these hermit/monks. (See the *Life of St. Anthony*,[1] written by the great Alexandrian bishop St. Athanasius, for an account of the extraordinary feats of self-denial and mortification of the flesh practiced by Anthony.) Before long it came to be felt that a communal life, not a solitary life, would be safer and better for such ascetics. This retreat from an eremitic to a cenobitic monasticism was a retreat from extreme to moderate asceticism—from an asceticism which, in its extremity, may have been influenced by Gnosticism to an asceticism that was more consistently Christian.

It should be noted that the great Father of the Church, St. Augustine (354–430), had been the follower of a more or less Gnostic religion, Manichaeism, prior to his conversion to Catholicism at about the age of thirty. Manichaeism held that the human body, being a material thing, is evil, and that all sexual conduct, including intercourse between husband and wife, is sinful. It can be argued, and often has been argued, that Augustine's Catholic views on sex were more than a little influenced by his earlier Manichaean views. It should be noted, however, that his Manichaean views did not hinder him from living a sexually active life during his Manichaean years; he didn't renounce sex and turn to a monastic way of life until he turned to Catholicism.

At first glance Manichaeism seems to have had a stricter attitude toward sex than did Catholicism. For the former held that all sex is sinful, even within marriage; while the latter taught that only sex outside of marriage is sinful, sex between husband and wife being quite licit, even mandatory. In practice, however, Manichaeism was quite tolerant of sex; for, since our lives were lived in evil bodies, we could not help but sin all day long; hence sex was sinful, but so were eating and drinking. Sex between boyfriend and girlfriend (Augustine's case) was no more sinful than sex between husband and wife.

The Manichaeans were divided into two groups: a small elite of leaders (the *perfecti*) and a large majority of followers (the *audi-*

[1] An English translation of this was published by TAN Books and Publishers in 1995 under the title *St. Anthony of the Desert.*

tores). It was only the former of these two groups of whom abstention from sex was demanded. Augustine was one of the *auditores*.

It should also be noted that there was a long tradition of pre-Christian asceticism in the Greek world, this asceticism being most famously exhibited in the Cynic school of philosophy, dating from about 400 BC. It is likely however that a non-philosophical tradition of Greek asceticism predated the Cynics.

The name of the Cynics comes from the Greek word for "dog," and this for one of two reasons: either because the Cynics used to gather at the Athenian stoa called the White Dog, or because, as we will see in a moment, they lived like dogs. My guess is that they were called dogs for both reasons.

The Cynics believed in living according to nature, and by "according to nature" they meant "as much as possible without the aid of man-made things or conventions." Hence they tried to live without money or houses or cooked food. Ideally they would have walked about naked instead of covering themselves in man-made garments. On this point, however, they compromised, covering their nakedness with a single old, tattered, dirty cloak. They went shoeless. They relieved themselves in public, as did dogs. They found nothing objectionable about having sex in public; after all, sex is a quite natural thing; why should anybody be ashamed? The most famous of all Cynics, Diogenes, used to masturbate in public. They did not consider themselves to be citizens of any particular city or state; for boundary lines between cities or states are man-made things. Instead they thought of themselves as citizens of the world.

Apart from sexual conduct, and apart from relieving themselves in public, Christian monks and nuns may be thought of as a continuation, a modified continuation, in Christian times of the pagan asceticism of the Cynics.

6

Sexual Motives

Another fascinating glimpse at the way early Christians thought of sex and sexuality can be found in a letter from Pope Gregory I (Gregory the Great) written in the early 600s to Augustine of Canterbury (not to be confused with St. Augustine of Hippo, the Father of the Church mentioned just above). Augustine of Canterbury, the missionary sent by Pope Gregory to England to convert the natives to Catholicism, wrote to the pope asking his advice on a number of matters. One of the questions posed by Augustine was this:

> May a man enter church after relations with his wife before he has washed? Or receive the sacred mystery of Communion? These uncouth English people require guidance on all these matters.[1]

Pope Gregory's answer to the question was:

> Lawful intercourse should be for the procreation of offspring, and not for mere pleasure; to obtain children, and not to satisfy lust. But if any man is not moved by a desire for pleasure, but only by a desire for children, he is to be left to his own judgment either as to entering church, or to receiving the Communion of the Body and Blood of our Lord; for we have no right to debar one who does not yield to the fires of temptation. But when lust takes the place of desire for children, the mere act

[1] Bede, *A History of the English Church and People* (Penguin Books, 1968), pp. 76-77.

> of union becomes something that the pair have cause to regret; and although the holy teachings give them permission, yet this carries a warning with it. For when the Apostle Paul said: "If they cannot contain, let them marry," he at once added, "I speak this by permission, and not of commandment." This concession makes it lawful, yet not good; so when he spoke of permission, he indicated that it was not blameless.[2]

To us moderns—and not just to secularized non-Christian moderns but also to genuinely Catholic men and women living in the modern world—Pope Gregory's apparent assumption that there are only two motives for sexual intercourse, desire for offspring and desire for carnal pleasure, seems very odd. Was Gregory unaware of romantic or erotic love? Hadn't he heard that lovers, whether joined in a marital union or not, are often driven to the sexual act by something that is neither a desire for pleasure nor a desire for children? Rather it is a desire for complete union—a union of bodies, to be sure, but also of hearts and minds and spirits; a desire to escape their isolated individualities and merge themselves in a higher unity, a third something that is better and higher than their individual selves.

Could it be that Pope Gregory, along with many other Catholic thinkers who reflected on sexual motivation over the centuries, was unduly influenced by Plato? Almost from the beginning Christian thought was strongly influenced by Plato's philosophy. Signs of this influence are perhaps found as early as in the writings of St. Paul, especially when the Apostle contrasts "spirit" and "flesh." An important feature of Plato's philosophy is his psychological theory, that the soul (*psyche*) has three parts or elements: (a) Reason, the highest part, which should always be in command of a person's conduct; (b) "Spirit," the middle part, which causes us to desire challenges, difficulties, obstacles to be overcome[3]; and

---

[2] Bede, Ibid, p. 81.

[3] The "spirit" spoken of by Plato (in English translation) is not to be confused with the spirit of spirituality or the spirit of immateriality. Rather, it is

(c) Appetite, the lowest part, which causes us to desire pleasure—and this means, among other things, that it causes us to desire sex. Reason is our uniquely human part, something we do not share with the lower animals. Spirit and Appetite are our animal parts; and of these two Spirit has some dignity, for it motivates us to actions that are often selfless and even heroic; whereas Appetite, an egoistic thing, is quite without dignity.

These Platonic notions gained great currency among ancient thinkers, who routinely spoke of sexual desire as a base appetite, something that tend to pull us in the direction of animality, and not the best kind of animality at that. Early Christianity, which inherited much of the intellectual legacy of the classical world, quite naturally inherited the notion that sex is an animalistic thing, hence a vile thing. How strange that such a vile thing should be found in a human being, who is made in the image and likeness of God. Its vileness may be overcome in a sexual act motivated by a wish for offspring, for such a wish is in accordance with God's command that we increase and multiply. But apart from this wish the desire for sexual pleasure remains vile, and when the desire is found outside of marriage its vileness only aggravates its sinfulness.

Very interestingly, Plato in his *Symposium* offers some very different thoughts about sexual desire. There he speaks of romantic love—more correctly, he has some of the characters in the dialogue speak of romantic love. (It must be noted that the kind of romantic love they speak of is not love between a man and a woman. No, it is the pederastic love felt by an adult man for a good-looking teenage boy. This species of homosexuality was very common among upper-class Greeks of Plato's day.) Romantic love is a love of beauty, the lowest stage of a ladder of love which, if climbed all the way to the top, eventuates in a love of Absolute Beauty or Absolute Goodness. In Plato's thought beauty and goodness are inseparable; they are either different names for the same thing or two sides of the same coin; wherever one is present, so also is the

---

like the spirit of team spirit or the spirit of a spirited defense or offense. It is the spirit of the energetic and adventuresome man.

other. In Plato's system this Absolute Goodness/Beauty is roughly equivalent to God in the Christian system. And so, if we make Plato speak Christian-wise, he is saying that romantic love is the lowest rung of the ladder that leads eventually to love of God; it is a foreshadowing of love of God. Not many lovers go all the way to the top. Many, overcome by their animal desire for sexual pleasure, never get beyond merely sexual love.

Many Christian philosophers and theologians approved of this Platonic notion that we humans have a natural desire for God and that this God-desire first manifests itself in our love, often a very mistaken love, for lower things. For example, St. Augustine, who in his *Confessions* wrote, "You have made us for yourself, O Lord, and our hearts are restless until they rest in you." But I'm unaware of any Christian thinker, at least in the first millennium AD, who followed Plato in treating romantic love as the first step on a ladder leading to love of God. Even Augustine, who may well have been romantically in love with his early girlfriend, does not do this. He regards sexual desire as a low, animal appetite.

Plato is a tremendous treasure-house of brilliant ideas. Unfortunately, however, not all of these ideas are logically consistent with one another.

Someplace in his long philosophical poem, *De Rerum Naturam*, the Roman poet-philosopher Lucretius (a disciple of the Greek philosopher Epicurus, and a first century BC contemporary of Caesar and Cicero) says that men and women who are deeply in love with one another are always disappointed and saddened after sexual intercourse. For what they want in sex is not simply sexual pleasure. No, serious lovers of this kind want complete union. During the sexual act they briefly experience the feeling, or rather the illusion, of complete union. But after the act they find that they are not unified, they are not a single being. Instead they are once again two persons, two separate egos. And this leaves them unhappy.

It was not until the twentieth century that Catholicism acknowledged the legitimacy of this "unitive" function of sexual intercourse—of course legitimizing it only in connection with sexual relations between husband and wives, not with regard to unmarried lovers; and even in the case of husbands and wives legitimizing it only when their acts of "unitive" love did not involve contraception.

The fact that Catholicism has paid relatively little attention to the unitive (or mad-passionate) motive for sexual intercourse is probably connected with the fact that the most famous cases of this kind of love, at any rate the most famous cases in literature, have taken place outside of marriage. Think of the following instances:

- Dido and Aeneas
- Caesar and Cleopatra
- Antony and Cleopatra
- Lancelot and Guinevere
- Tristan and Iseult
- Madame Bovary
- Anna Karenina

The pattern or basic plot of stories like this is the same in every case. (a) A man and a woman fall madly in love with one another. A variation of this pattern may be that only one of the pair, usually the woman, falls *madly* in love; e.g., Dido or Madame Bovary. (b) Some serious obstacle prevents them from marrying one another. Usually, but not always, this obstacle is the fact that one of them is already married, or perhaps both of them. But the obstacle might be something else, e.g., Aeneas's god-given mission to go to Italy. (c) A great variety of dramatic consequences follow from this dilemma.

In addition to famous works of literature, tales of mad-passionate love abound in second- and third-rate novels, and have formed the plots of a thousand movies. Rarely are these works of great artistic merit. Usually they are sentimental love stories. But they have had a great influence on the world, an influence with which Catholicism cannot be totally pleased. For one, this influence often leads to a sentimental-romantic belief that diminishes the likelihood of a successful marriage; a belief that somewhere in the world, among the world's billions of people, there is a person whom fate has destined to be one's perfect soulmate. And so Jill falls madly in love with Jack, thinking he is THE PERFECT

ONE, and she marries him. Well, as time passes she learns that he does not fit that description; he is not her perfect soulmate. At this point one of two things happens: (a) either Jill finally grows up, realizes there is no such thing as THE PERFECT ONE, and settles down to make the best of her imperfect marriage to Jack; or (b) Jill resists growing up, decides that Jack has been a great mistake, and that she should keep trying to find THE PERFECT ONE.

Further, this sentimental-passionate belief encourages a kind of practical atheism. Marriage to this THE PERFECT ONE, we feel, will be a kind of Heaven on Earth. We will not need a Heaven after death. We will not need God. Or perhaps it is the other way around. Maybe it is disbelief in God's existence, or at least strong doubt as to that existence, that gives plausibility to the idea that THE PERFECT ONE is waiting for us. If we cannot have God, we can have our perfect soul-mate, and he/she will be just as good.

In any case, it is not surprising that the Catholic Church, when thinking about the motives for sexual love between husband and wife, kept its focus on the desire for pleasure (in itself a good thing, but at the same time a temptation to a variety of serious sins) and on the desire for children (a very good thing). Only after many centuries did the Church tell us that the passionate desire for marital "union" is also a good thing—and indeed has been a good thing all along, even though it did not have a good press. A fine expression of the unitive function of the conjugal act is found in Pope Paul VI's encyclical *Humanae Vitae*, in a section titled "Union and Procreation."

> This particular doctrine [that every conjugal act must be of a non-contraceptive character], often expounded by the Magisterium of the Church, is based on the inseparable connection, established by God, which man on his own initiative may not break, between the unitive significance and the procreative significance which are both inherent to the marriage act.
>
> The reason is that the fundamental nature of the marriage act, while uniting husband and wife in

> the closest intimacy, also renders them capable of generating new life—and this as a result of laws written into the actual nature of man and of woman. And if each of these essential qualities, the unitive and the procreative, is preserved, the use of marriage fully retains its sense of true mutual love and its ordination to the supreme responsibility of parenthood to which man is called.[4]

In summary, then, we can say that early Christianity had two ideals of sexual morality: (1) a higher and more demanding ideal of chaste celibacy or lifelong abstention from sex, an ideal that monks and nuns and priests were expected to live up to; and (2) a lower and less demanding ideal of chaste monogamy.

This lower ideal was not that much lower than the higher ideal. It was substantially the same except that in the case of married couples the higher ideal was modified so as to accommodate the duty that married couples have: to produce, or at least *try* to produce, offspring. The only allowable sexual intercourse was sex with one's spouse.

Unmarried persons—whether these were not-yet-married persons, or widowed persons, or married persons who for some reason or other were not living with their spouses—were to abstain from sex altogether. And if you were married, the ideal was to have sex for the sake of begetting children, not merely for the sake of carnal pleasure. However, sex simply for the sake of pleasure, though imperfect, was morally allowable provided you did nothing to prevent conception. Forms of sexual contact that resulted in the husband's semen being deposited anywhere except in his wife's vagina were banned.

All other sex was prohibited for both married and unmarried persons: no adultery was allowed, likewise no onanism (masturbation), and of course no homosexuality.

---

[4] Section 12 of *Humanae Vitae*. My quote comes from a book by Dietrich von Hildebrand, *Love, Marriage, and the Catholic Conscience* (Sophia Institute Press, 1998), which includes the full text of HV. The words I quote appear on page 119 of the book.

In the twenty-first century this remains, with only small modifications, the teaching of the Catholic Church. There have been two modifications.

(1) Catholicism now recognizes a third motive for marital intercourse in addition to the two motives acknowledged by Pope Gregory I (carnal pleasure and a desire for offspring). This third motive is a "unitive" motive: a wish to strengthen the bond of affection between husband and wife. This is a morally allowable motive, indeed it is an admirable motive, provided of course that it does not interfere with the possibility of conception. The Church has not retreated from its traditional idea that God's primary aim in endowing us with sexual capacities is procreation.

(2) The other modification is that Catholicism now acknowledges the moral legitimacy of a married couple using a kind of birth control in order to better "space" children—provided the "birth control" in question is natural family planning (NFP), which is to say periodic abstinence. The ancient prohibition of artificial birth control or *coitus interruptus* remains in place.

Part II

The Protestant Sexual Revolution

The Protestant Reformation of the sixteenth century was a generalized rebellion against Catholicism. The rebellion involved many things, among them the following: a rejection of the papacy; an affirmation that the Bible alone is the rule of faith; an affirmation of predestination; a corresponding denial of free will; and an assertion that the individual is saved by faith alone, not by works.

But the Reformation also involved a sexual revolution, a revolution that was relatively permissive when compared to the Catholic sexual standards that preceded it—and it is this revolution that I will speak about in the next four chapters.

Compared to the sexual revolution of the last part of the twentieth century, a revolution that is still in progress in the first part of the twenty-first century, this old Protestant sexual revolution seems an awfully tame thing in its permissiveness. For the makers of the earlier revolution—Luther, Calvin, and a host of other reformers—were believers in chastity, though not in what I called earlier in this book hyper-chastity. Luther, Calvin, and almost every other notable reformer was—or at least became in the course of the Reformation—a married man, something a Catholic priest could never do.

By contrast, our modern sexual revolutionaries, though they usually believe in a certain amount of *sexual prudence* (they say, for instance, that unmarried heterosexuals should take precautions against unwanted pregnancy and that everybody, heterosexuals and homosexuals, should take precautions against disease), they have no belief in chastity. They do not see chastity as a virtue. If anything, they see it as a vice, or at least as foolishness.

What do I have in mind when I speak of the Protestant Sexual Revolution? Three things above all: (1) the end of monasticism, (2) the end of mandatory priestly celibacy, and (3) the end of the idea that marriage is indissoluble.

7

The End of Monasticism

Wherever Protestantism triumphed, monasticism came to an end. Monks and nuns, men and women committed to lives of celibate chastity, were invited to leave their monasteries and convents; and if they did not wish to leave, they were forcibly ejected from their homes, which were closed down.

This was not because the people and rulers in the Protestant parts of Europe no longer believed in the asceticism that had characterized the preceding Catholic centuries; or at least it was not purely and simply because of that. Much of the motive on the part of political authorities for closing monasteries and convents, probably even *most* of the motive, was a lust for land and other wealth (e.g., furniture and silverware) on the part of rulers and their aristocratic allies. Europe had not yet become a predominantly bourgeois world, that is, a world that is socially, economically, and politically dominated by the classes of merchants and manufacturers and lawyers. Land—not industrial capital, money, stocks, or bonds—was still the principal form of wealth. And so monasteries and convents were rich, for they owned great amounts of land, much of it having been gained from the wilderness by the hard work of monks and nuns, the remainder having been donated by pious laypersons in the expectation that the monks and nuns would pray for the souls of the donors after the donors had died. The Reformation involved an enormous transfer of wealth from religious orders and congregations to the monarchs and upper classes of northern Europe.

In the Catholic scheme of things, which included the belief that most of those who would eventually end up in Heaven would in the meantime—in the interval, that is, between death and ultimate arrival in Heaven—serve a time of finite probation and punishment in Purgatory, it made sense to pray for the souls of the dead. For, with the exception of a small number of saints who had proceeded directly to Heaven upon dying, the souls of the dead were in Purgatory; that is where your friends and relatives had gone—provided of course that they had not gone directly to Hell. These souls needed the prayers of the living to help shorten their time in Purgatory. For monks and nuns, praying for the dead was something like a full-time job. If monks and nuns were not available to pray for the dead, countless millions of souls would be forced to endure the pains of Purgatory far longer than necessary. And so, if I were a rich man, it made sense for me to leave a great amount of wealth (that is, land) to a monastery or convent on the understanding that the monks or nuns would do a lot of heavy-duty praying for my soul. Instead of spending, say, ten thousand years in Purgatory, perhaps, thanks to these prayers, I would get out and go to Heaven in ten or twenty years.

But Protestantism did away with the belief in Purgatory, and so there was no need for anybody to pray for the souls of the dead; for at the moment of death the soul of the dead person passed directly either to Heaven or to Hell. If to the former place, the departed soul had no need of prayers; if to the latter, prayers would be of no help. So when the monasteries closed down, and no more monks and nuns were available to pray for the souls of the dead, it did not matter to Protestants. Such prayers for the dead were useless. In any case, kings and princes and lords and ladies were quite happy to lay their hands on the immense real estate holdings of the closed monasteries and convents, not to mention their often abundant silverware.

If the question be asked, "What came first, the disbelief in Purgatory or the closing of the monasteries and convents?" the answer should probably be, "They happened simultaneously." It seems to have been a case of mutual causation; the development of each prompted the development of the other. If there are no souls in Purgatory needing prayers from the living, what is the point of having these thousands and thousands of monasteries and convents? If on the other hand we wish to seize this immense amount of monastic and conventual wealth, we will be able to do so with easier consciences if we no longer have to believe that there are souls in Purgatory waiting for the prayers of monks and nuns.

Was that the whole story? Were the convents and monasteries closed purely and simply because of royal and aristocratic greed? No. This was certainly a large part of the story, but not the whole story. If it had been, there would have been widespread resistance to the closing of the monasteries, not just on the part of the monks and nuns themselves, but on the part of ordinary lay people, those who received no material profit from the closings. True, there was some resistance. In England, for instance, there was a great though short-lived resistance to King Henry VIII's transformation of the English church from a Catholic to a Protestant church, a transformation that involved the closing of every monastery and convent in England. By and large, however, in England, Scotland, Northern Germany, Holland, and Scandinavia, the abolition of monasticism went rather smoothly; it was accepted by the people.

It was accepted, however, not because Christian people had lost their appreciation for the ascetic life that had characterized monastic and conventual life. If anything, it was accepted for just the opposite reason. It must be kept in mind that the Reformation was not the result of a decline in Christian feeling in Western Europe. Just the opposite; it was the result of an intensification of Christian feeling; a kind of Christian revival. Beginning a generation or two following the "Black Death" (the bubonic plague that killed what may have been a third of the population of Western Europe in the middle years of the fourteenth century), there was a great upsurge in lay piety and devotion.

For centuries Catholicism had been without question a two-tier religion. If you wanted to find examples of full-fledged Christianity you had to look at monks, nuns, and (to a lesser degree) parish priests. Outside of these three groups, among ordinary laypersons, you would not expect to find, except in exceedingly rare instances, anything more than a watered-down Christianity—a Christianity that was generously blended with moral laxity on the one hand and vulgar superstition on the other. The two tiers were held together in a single religion by common beliefs, common sacraments, and a common ecclesiastical establishment, this establishment being controlled and operated by the higher of the two tiers. But after the Black Death something changed. In the second half of the fourteenth century and throughout the fifteenth century, millions of ordinary people, lay men and lay women, especially those living in Germany and the Low Countries, increasingly aspired to be full-fledged Christians. The gap between elite Christians (monks and nuns and priests) and ordinary Christians narrowed. If these ordinary Christians rarely achieved full sanctity, they at least *attempted* to achieve it, and in doing so they developed a vivid awareness of high religious and moral standards; and they were then able to use these high standards to judge the religious inadequacies found in many persons belonging to the higher tier—monks and nuns and priests and bishops and popes.

When in the first quarter of the sixteenth century Luther came along and suggested that the Christianity of the Roman Church was not true Christianity, this suggestion tallied with the feelings of many lay Catholics, and these pious lay Catholics agreed with Luther and his fellow Reformers that to repudiate the church of Rome was to open the door to a better and more genuine Christianity. When the convents and monasteries were closed, pious laypersons—who for a century and more had believed that a fully Christian life could be lived in the "world," that is, outside of monastic institutions, and could perhaps be lived even better outside these institutions—were not horrified. They did not say to themselves what they might have said a few centuries earlier, "If there are no more monks and nuns, there will be no more true Christians." Instead they said to themselves, "The convents and monasteries are superfluous. You do not need to be a monk or a nun to be a good Christian. You can be a good Christian even while being a lay person. And perhaps you can be an even better person, for lots of these monks and nuns are *not* good Christians. They are ne'er-do-wells living off the fat of their huge estates."

The abolition of monasticism, then, did not involve the abolition of asceticism, for asceticism was seen by pious laypersons as part and parcel of the Christian life. So had it been seen by

Catholics prior to the Reformation and so was it seen by Protestants (or at least by many of them) during the Reformation. In his classic work of sociology, history, and economics, *The Protestant Ethic and the Spirit of Capitalism*,[1] Max Weber makes a distinction between two kinds of asceticism, "other-worldly" and "inner-worldly." The former is the asceticism of the monks and nuns, the latter the asceticism of pious laypersons. The former was Catholic, the latter Protestant. More specifically, the latter was typical of the most thoroughly Protestant wing of Protestantism ("the Protestantism of the Protestant religion," as Edmund Burke later called it), that is, Baptists, Congregationalists (Independents), Presbyterians, Quakers, etc., as contrasted with Lutherans and Anglicans, who occupied a position that was, with regard to lay asceticism, closer to old-fashioned Catholicism than to thoroughgoing Protestantism. A general name for this "more thoroughly Protestant wing of Protestantism" would be Puritanism. Although all of Reformation Protestantism had a tendency toward inner-worldly asceticism, this kind of asceticism could be found at full strength only among Puritans. Weber sees this asceticism as a descendant with modification of the other-worldly asceticism of the medieval monks and nuns. Instead of practicing asceticism behind the closed doors of a monastery or convent, these new ascetics lived their ascetic lives in the midst of "the world."

But if these Puritans did not give up the old ideal of Christian asceticism, they did abandon one section of the traditional ideal, namely the life of celibate chastity. There were two principal reasons for this. First, if you were going to live in "the world," this worldly life would involve marriage and children, hence sexual intercourse between husband and wife. Second, a life of celibate chastity, that is, a life in which one never gave in to the sexual urges that were part and parcel of our human nature, at least of the corrupted human nature that has been ours since the Fall of Adam and Eve—this celibate life was, as Protestants saw it, an unnatural life. If God has given us these urges, these powerful sexual

---

[1] English translation by Talcott Parsons first published in 1930; reprinted in 1992 by Routledge.

urges, it must be that God wants us to make use of them. To refuse, as did monks and nuns and priests, to use your sexual organs as God and nature meant them to be used, namely to produce children, is not a way of serving God; it is a way of defying him.

Of course in providing us with a capacity for sexual intercourse, God does not want us to use this capacity in an unrestricted way. He has surrounded this capacity with reasonable prohibitions: no fornication, no adultery, no masturbation, no homosexuality, no polygamy. But God has allowed us, indeed has commanded us, to have chaste sexual relations with our spouse. Such was the Protestant-Puritan view.

Since sexual relations within the boundaries of monogamous marriage are natural, the deliberate refusal of marriage, it seemed to Protestants, is unnatural. And since our natural (and God-given) sexual urges are powerful things, if they are not given legitimate outlet there is a very good chance they will seek illegitimate outlets. And thus there developed among Protestants something that might be called "the myth of Catholic clerical immorality," a myth that contained the following articles of belief:

- that illicit sex abounded among monks and nuns in pre-Reformation days and still abounds in Catholic regions of Europe;
- that monasteries and convents were (and still are) hotbeds of sexual immorality and homosexual perversion;
- that nuns were (and still are) often made pregnant by priests who visit convents to say Mass or to hear confessions;
- that many pregnant nuns underwent (and still undergo) abortions;
- that infanticide was (and still is) not unknown in these convents;
- that newly killed infants were (are) buried in the backyards of convents.

This very common Protestant belief in the gross sexual immorality of Catholics who had taken vows of chaste celibacy endured for centuries, and it eventually crossed the ocean to the new world of North America. A classic example of this was *Awful Disclosures of Maria Monk*, a ferociously anti-Catholic book (written in the

1830s) that purported to be an autobiographical tale of a young woman who, having become a nun, eventually escaped from a convent in Montreal. She reported that she had witnessed, and to some degree had even participated in, the horrors that were widely believed by Protestants to take place in Catholic convents.

At all events, monasticism, which for more than one thousand years had helped shape the moral, intellectual, religious, and economic life of Europe, suddenly—in the second quarter of the sixteenth century—was wiped off the map of great sections of northwestern Europe.

8

The End of a Celibate Priesthood

A life of chaste celibacy had always been an informal ideal for Catholic parish priests, but in the eleventh century it was made mandatory by papal decree. The Reformation did away with this ancient ideal. The new ideal, the Protestant ideal, was that a parish priest (or pastor or minister) should be a married man. There were a number of reasons for this new ideal.

1. It is God's intention that all men and women, including priests/ministers, should marry. Two things make this clear: (a) the fact that God has given sexual organs and strong sexual desires to all humans; and (b) the examples given by the saints of the Old Testament, all of whom were married.

2. The belief (noted in the preceding chapter) that celibacy is an unnatural state and that those who attempt it are in grave danger of falling into sexual immorality and perversion. Hence there is something unnatural—even dangerous—about an unmarried minister.

3. If your local minister is married, he will have little or no motive for seducing your wife or your daughters.

4. A minster with a wife and children would be far "closer" to his parishioners or congregants. He would be living a life very like the lives *they* are living. He could understand them better than a celibate priest ever could. He could counsel them more wisely.

5. Protestantism had revived the old Christian idea of the "priesthood of all believers." It is not that Catholicism had repudiated this idea, but for all practical purposes it had allowed it to become dormant. The Protestant revival of the old idea meant that there was no longer any great gap between clergy and laity—no "on-

tological gap," so to speak, as if priest and layperson belonged to two different species of human being. They were now on the same level; and if the Protestant minster was commonly viewed as a religiously superior or more elevated person, this was not because he was a superior kind of being; it was because he was presumed to be more learned in the Bible and more virtuous in his conduct.

There were some inconveniences, however, in having a non-celibate priesthood. For one thing it was more expensive to support a priest/minister plus his wife and children than to support a minister alone. For another, it wasn't enough that the minister himself live a scandal-free life; it was almost equally important that his wife and children live in a scandal-free manner. Whatever the costs of having a married clergy, however, Protestantism felt that the price was well worth paying.

In the eyes of suspicious Protestants, Catholic parish priests, having done the foolish and unnatural thing of renouncing marriage, were exposed to temptations similar to those faced by monks and nuns. The victims of the parish priest's lust would rarely be nuns, for as a parish priest he had relatively little contact with nuns, who for the most part lived in cloisters. It was far more probable that his sex partners (victims) would be the wives and daughters of parishioners. And while the parish priest might be less likely than monks to have sodomite relations with other priests, he would be more likely to have such relations with boys in the parish. If you were a married layman in a Catholic parish, you'd have to be careful that your local priest did not corrupt your wife or your daughters or your sons. Such was a common Protestant belief.

Since the old hatred between Catholics and Protestants has largely passed away nowadays, not many Protestants today continue to hold the old-fashioned view that the typical Catholic priest will at some point in his career violate his vow of chastity. But for those who still do hold this view, their view got a tremendous corroboration with the revelations of priestly sexual molestation of teenagers, mainly boys, that came to widespread public notice in the early years of the twenty-first century. If strongly anti-Catholic Protestants from the 16th, 17th, 18th, and 19th centuries had been able to look far enough into the future and had seen the twenty-first-century scandal, they would have said, "See, we told you so." And if we had informed them that only a very small percentage of Catholic priests had been involved in this scandal, they would have answered, "Only a small percentage that you *know* about."

9

Freedom to Divorce and Remarry

Catholicism had taught, and still teaches, that marriage is indissoluble. It can be ended only by the death of one of the parties. The pre-Christian religion of the Jews had permitted divorce-and-remarriage in some circumstances. But Jesus banned this—at least as Catholicism understood the teaching of Jesus. Protestantism disagreed. In doing so it relied on two verses in the Gospel of Matthew. In these verses Jesus, when banning divorce-and-remarriage, makes an exception in the case of sexual misconduct. In those places he says, or at least *seems* to say, that a man may divorce his wife if she is guilty of adultery. (He does not say, however, that a woman may divorce her husband for adultery; at the same time neither does he bar a woman from initiating divorce for this reason.)

One of these verses is Matthew 5:32.

- This verse in the Authorized Version[1] is: "But I say unto you, that whosoever shall put away his wife, saving for the cause of fornication, causeth her to commit adultery: and whosoever shall marry her that is divorced committeth adultery."
- The Douay-Rheims Version[2] is almost identical: "But I say to you, that whosoever shall put away his wife, excepting for the cause of fornication, maketh her to commit adultery: and he that shall marry her that is put away, committeth adultery."

The other verse is Matthew 19:9.

- In the King James Version: "And I say to you, whosoever shall

[1] The King James Version (a Protestant translation) of the early seventeenth century.

[2] The Catholic translation from the same era as the King James Version.

put away his wife, except it be for fornication, and shall marry another, committeth adultery . . ."

- The Douay-Rheims Version has it word for word the same as the KJV.

In parallel passages in the Gospels of Luke and Mark, however, Jesus does *not* make this exception for adultery/fornication. He flatly bans divorce-and-remarriage; no exception allowed. In Mark the verse is at 10:11.

- King James Version: "And he saith unto them, Whosoever shall put away his wife and marry another, committeth adultery against her."
- The verse in the Douay-Rheims Version is word-for-word identical with the KJV except that the DRV says "to" where the KJV says "unto."

In Luke the parallel verse is at 16:18.

- In the King James Version: "Whosoever putteth away his wife, and marrieth another, committeth adultery: and whosoever marrieth her that is put away from her husband committeth adultery."
- In the Douay-Rheims Version: "Every one that putteth away his wife, and marrieth another, committeth adultery: and he that marrieth her that is put away from her husband, committeth adultery."

So who has the correct report of the words of Jesus? Is it Matthew? Or is it Luke and Mark? It is more likely, far more likely in my opinion, that Luke and Mark have it right; and this for at a number of reasons.

1. For one, it is hard to believe that Mark and Luke would have failed to mention so important an exception to Jesus's no-divorce rule.

2. For another, the Luke/Mark report is consistent with the absolute rule against divorce that seems to have been accepted in the early Church.

3. Besides, it is reported (Matthew 19:10) that some disciples had a strong negative reaction to Jesus's teaching on divorce-and-remarriage, "If such is the case of a man with his wife," they said, "it is not expedient to marry." But if the teaching was the one that

seems to be found in Matthew, why would the disciples find it to be such a hard saying? For in that case, though it would have been somewhat stricter than the prevailing Jewish teaching, it would not have been shockingly strict. But if they found it to be shockingly strict, it must have been something strikingly different and far more difficult to bear than the prevalent teaching among Jews.

4. If Jesus made an exception for adultery, why would he not make further exceptions for other very serious offenses? If you were a wife, whom would you be more eager to divorce, a husband who from time to time went to bed with a woman who lives across town, or a husband who was in the habit of beating you black and blue every time he came home drunk? And if you were a man, whom would you be more eager to divorce, a wife who had been unfaithful on a single occasion ten years ago, or a wife you recently caught trying to poison you?

5. Besides, doesn't the adultery exception open the door for fraud? If husband and wife have mutually agreed that they would like to divorce for reasons having nothing to do with adultery, wouldn't they be able to lie to the judge? Even though no adultery may have been committed, couldn't the wife (or husband) say to the judge, "I caught my husband (or wife) in adultery," and couldn't the other spouse then say, "I confess, I did it"? Lying to the judge is very wrong, of course, but if divorce for adultery is allowed, an incentive to tell this lie is created.

But is it conceivable that Matthew would on his own initiative have amended the words of Jesus on so important a question? Can it be that Matthew, feeling that the revolutionary words of Jesus were too hard for ordinary Jewish Christians to bear, "improved" these words to make them less shocking? Very unlikely.

There is, however, a way to reconcile the two reports. The word that gets translated as "fornication" in the older translations of Matthew's controversial passage, and as "unchastity" in some newer translations—this Greek word is "porneia," a word which, while it suggests serious sexual impropriety, can be translated into English in a number of possible ways, "adultery" being one of them, "fornication" being another, "unchastity" being a third. It is possible that Matthew had in mind an improper sexual partnership that was intermediate between marriage and adultery; for example, a relationship of unmarried cohabitation (the kind of sexual relationship millions of young couples in the USA have today); or a relationship of concubinage.

It must further be kept in mind that the Gospel of Matthew, though written in Greek (as is every book of the New Testament), is generally believed to have been based on an earlier document written in Aramaic, the language probably spoken by Jesus. Therefore the Greek word ("porneia") translated into English as "fornication" and "adultery" and "unchastity" is a step away from the Aramaic word that Jesus actually used, and the English words are two steps away from the actual words of Jesus. It may be the case, and I think it very probably was the case, that Jesus (as quoted in Matthew) was saying something like this: "You may not divorce your wife—except in those cases in which your apparent wife is not your real wife; instead she is your live-in girlfriend or concubine." Am I correct about this? Who knows? In any case it is a hypothesis that allows us to reconcile the words found in Matthew not only with the parallel words found in Mark and Luke but with the practice of the early Church and the perennial teaching of the Catholic Church. So there are very good reasons for accepting this hypothesis.

Though the Catholic reading of the no-divorce teaching of Jesus is far more likely to be correct than the Protestant reading, for a long time the conflict of interpretations did not make much practical difference between the two rival religions. For a few centuries not many Protestants took advantage of the new right to divorce and remarry. Perhaps this was because not many Protestants committed adultery; or because society, which was quite unwilling to tolerate female adultery, was willing to tolerate a certain amount of male adultery, with the result that not many injured wives took the trouble to attempt to divorce their cheating husbands; or because not many men or women were willing to endure the shame of a public divorce proceeding; or perhaps for a combination of two or more of these reasons.

In any case, while Catholic societies had no divorces at all, Protestant societies had only a few. Both Catholics and Protestants took it for granted that marriage was a till-death-do-us-part kind of thing.

Even King Henry VIII of England, he of the six wives, the most famous multi-married Protestant in Europe, never got a divorce.

(1) His first marriage, that to Catherine of Aragon, ended not in divorce but in an annulment. After the pope refused to grant Henry the annulment he asked for, Henry broke with Rome, made the Church of England a non-Roman and non-papal church, and had his Protestant Archbishop of Canterbury (Thomas Cranmer) declare that Henry's marriage to Catherine had been null and void.

(2) His second marriage, to Anne Boleyn, ended not in divorce but in the death of the queen, who was tried and beheaded at the initiative of Henry, because (so Henry believed) she was guilty of adultery, an offense that counted as treason when committed by the wife of the king, hence deserving the death penalty. However, so angry was Henry with Anne that he had Archbishop Cranmer pronounce the marriage of Henry and Anne to be null and void. Poor unlucky Anne. Since her marriage to Henry had been declared null, then her "adultery" (if she had committed it) was not truly adultery, since she had never been married, and therefore it was not treason and not deserving of the death penalty. What is more, she was probably not guilty of the illicit sexual encounters with which she was charged.

(3) His third marriage, to Jane Seymour, ended not in divorce but in the death of the queen, who died twelve days after giving birth to the future king, Edward VI.

(4) His fourth marriage, to Anne of Cleves, was apparently never consummated and ended not in divorce but in annulment. Henry did not find this Anne physically attractive. (Oh the nerve of Henry, that grossly overweight man, to scorn anybody for lack of attractiveness!) The marriage to Anne, a German Protestant, had been arranged by Henry's right-hand man, Thomas Cromwell. As a result of Henry's disappointment, Cromwell fell from power and soon was put to death.

(5) His fifth marriage, to Catherine Howard, ended not in divorce but in the death of the queen, who was beheaded for the treasonous crime of adultery. In Catherine Howard's case, unlike

in Anne Boleyn's case, there seems to be no doubt that she had truly been unfaithful to the king. As in the case of Anne Boleyn, however, the marriage between Henry and Catherine was annulled just prior to Catherine's death; which meant that Catherine could not have committed adultery since, strictly speaking, she was not married to him.

(6) His final marriage was to Catherine Parr. The marriage began in 1543, and ended in 1547 with Henry's death.

It was not easy to be either Henry's wife or his employee.

If Henry VIII's preferred way of getting a new wife was to get rid of the old wife via decapitation or annulment, not divorce, Philip of Hesse[3] is another great example of a Reformation-era Protestant ruler who didn't believe in divorce even though he very much wanted to acquire a new wife.

Philip (1504–67) was the Landgrave (that is, the monarch) of the mid-size German principality of Hesse. Though he had grown up Catholic, he embraced the Protestant cause at about the age of twenty. He was one of the leading secular supporters of the Reformation in Germany, a notable leader in the Protestant effort, ultimately successful, to prevent the Holy Roman Emperor Charles V, a Catholic, from re-Catholicizing the Empire.

Philip wed in 1523, and a few weeks later commenced a career of adultery: according to his friend and protégée Martin Luther, Philip lived "constantly in a state of adultery and fornication." Philip was not happy with his wife, and so he began thinking of getting a new wife. But he had no wish to divorce his first wife, either because (a) he did not believe in divorce, or because (b) she had given him no grounds for divorce, not having committed adultery. Instead he wanted to be a Christian bigamist; he wanted to take a second wife while still married to the first. He argued that Old Testament figures had had two simultaneous wives (e.g., Jacob, who was married to both Rachel and Leah), apparently with God's permission; and that what was morally permissible for Old Testament saints must also be permissible for Christians. At

[3] The following account is largely reliant on the Wikipedia entry "Philip I, Landgrave of Hesse."

first Martin Luther was unwilling to condone this plan for bigamy. But later, after Philip—whose political and military support was very much needed by the Protestant cause—had won the support of two of the leading Reformers, Philip Melanchthon and Martin Bucer, the reluctant Luther came on board, giving Philip his green light. (Also giving approval, it should be noted, was his first wife.) And so Philip took a second wife while still being married to his first wife.

There was of course a danger that this might become a precedent in the Protestant world. If it had done so, this would have made for one further difference between Protestantism and Catholicism, that the former permitted bigamy while the latter did not. But the danger was never realized. Philip of Hesse was a unique case. No precedent was set. Except for this single anomalous case, Protestantism was as opposed to bigamy as was Catholicism.

It should be noted that Philip fathered nineteen legitimate children, ten with his first wife, nine with his second. Whatever Biblical commandments he may have violated, he clearly obeyed the one that tells us to "increase and multiply."

In pre-modern Catholic societies, though there were no *de jure* divorces, there were more than a few *de facto* divorces. For one, there were annulments. Legally speaking, an annulment was not a divorce: it was an official declaration by the Church that the apparent marriage had never been a true marriage. Some impediment had stood in the way at the time of the wedding: for example, the partners were too closely related[4]; or one of the partners had been compelled to marry without giving his or her genuine consent; or one of the partners was married to a still-living spouse; or one of the partners was too young at the moment of the wedding, therefore unable to give consent; or one of the partners was unwilling or unable to consummate the marriage. At all events, if in a

---

[4] In the Middle Ages the rules of the Catholic Church prohibited marriage between cousins, even relatively distant cousins. If you were a prince and you wanted to divorce your princess, you would research your family tree; and you might then discover that your disliked wife is a cousin within the prohibited degrees of kinship; and so your bishop or the pope would have good reason to declare your marriage null and void. And thus you were free to marry again.

Catholic country you were determined to get rid of your spouse and free yourself to marry a new spouse, there was a pretty good chance that you could find a good reason for getting an annulment. Nowadays even ordinary people can find this reason and can be given, and often are given (especially in the USA), annulments, thus freeing them to marry a new spouse. But until the second half of the twentieth century, getting an annulment was rare, troublesome, and often expensive. And so for most practical purposes annulments were limited to Catholics of royal, aristocratic, or high bourgeois status. Beginning in the second half of the twentieth century, however, the privilege of getting an annulment was open to all Catholics, regardless of their social or economic status; at least this has been the case in the United States of America, where many, perhaps even most, annulments became in effect "Catholic divorces."

But in the old days, I mean a few centuries ago, what did Catholic peasants and other poor people do when they wished to get rid of their spouses and find a new spouse? The annulment process was too much trouble for them, and too expensive; that was reserved for the higher classes. And what did ordinary Protestants do, people whose spouses had not committed adultery, or whose adulteries were not provable, but who were nonetheless quite unbearable as marriage partners, who were nearly impossible to live with?

There is not much of a historical record of this kind of thing since hardly anybody created written accounts of such developments. But it is easy to guess. Both Catholic and Protestant poor people in unhappy marriages had two choices. They could, on the one hand, simply grin and bear it; that is, they could remain in their miserable marriages; and this is probably what happened in most instances. Or they could simply walk away. They could abandon the marriage without passing through the formality of Catholic annulment or Protestant divorce. And after that, if they were lucky, they could find a new spouse-like partner; a quasi-wife or quasi-husband.

But how would such people be treated by their local Catholic priest or Protestant minister? Would they be allowed to receive

Communion? Would their babies be baptized? Would they be given a church burial? It must have depended on the local pastor. If he was a stickler for legal precision, he would treat them as a couple living in sin, he would regard their babies as bastards, and he would refuse to give the couple a full church burial. But if he was less of a purist and strongly inclined to avoid trouble, he would look the other way. After a certain decent interval had passed, he would treat the couple pretty much the way he would treat other couples in his parish, easing his conscience by telling himself that he could not be *absolutely sure* their union was not legitimate. Or someday he could ask them, "Are you two really and truly married to one another?" And they could answer, "Yes"—perhaps because they were lying, or more likely because they were giving what they erroneously believed to be a correct answer. After all, poor, uneducated people like this could not be expected to know the details of the law of marriage. Who could blame her ignorance if an uneducated woman believed that the man she had been living with for a few years, and by whom she had had children, was her husband? And who could blame the ignorance of an uneducated man who believed that the woman he had been living with for a few years, and who had given birth to his children, was his wife?

For a few centuries nothing much changed in either the Catholic or Protestant worlds with regard to the permanence of marriage. They both held that they abided by the teaching of Jesus. That is, Catholicism held that marriage is absolutely indissoluble, as Jesus had declared (in Mark and Luke), while Protestant had held that marriage is *almost* indissoluble, allowing for the single exception that Jesus had allowed (in Matthew).

Little changed with regard to practice, but something had changed in principle. Thanks to annulment (which was often in the past, as it often is today, little more than a legal fiction), and thanks to turning an occasional blind eye, Catholicism was able to say to itself and to the outside world, "We hold that marriage—a true marriage, a valid marriage—can be dissolved by nothing other than death." Catholicism had, at least in principle if not always in practice, held to the principle that marriage is indissoluble.

But Protestantism had opened the door to divorce. True, it had opened it only a crack: only for one fault, adultery. But the opening was there. The door was no longer completely shut. And if it could be opened on account of adultery, why could it not be pushed further open on account of things just as bad as adultery, or even worse? What about wife-beating? What about child abuse? What about habitual drunkenness? What about a life of crime? What about desertion? What about a refusal to support the family? If Jesus (as Protestants believed) thought adultery was bad enough to allow an exception to be made to the no-divorce rule, isn't it reasonable (Protestants might ask) to believe that he thought other exceptions should also be made?

"But," it would be objected, "he actually and very specifically mentioned adultery as an exception while not mentioning other exceptions."

"Yes," it might be replied, "but the fact that he mentioned only one exception does not mean that he was ruling out all other exceptions.[5] It was enough that he gave the hint. He was clearly implying that marriage is *not* indissoluble. When he says (in Matthew) 'except for adultery,' should we not read this to mean 'except for adultery . . . and comparable evils'?"

In the nineteenth century some Protestant countries (Britain, Scandinavia, the Protestant parts of Germany) and many American states began taking seriously what they saw as the reasonable implications of what they understood to be Jesus' adultery exception. With time, exceptions mounted up. First there was *this* "good reason" for divorce, and then there was *that* "good reason," until by the middle of the twentieth century in the United States, there were many "good reasons."

Beginning in the late 1960s in the United States, so-called "no-fault" divorce laws were introduced in one state after another until this finally became the law in every state. Prior to no-fault divorce laws, an American court would grant a divorce only if one of the parties was found to be guilty of a "fault," that is, some

[5] Similarly, the fact that the gospels contain no record of Jesus specifically and explicitly condemning homosexuality and arson does not imply that Jesus was giving his okay to homosexuality and arson.

marital misbehavior specified in law and grievous enough to justify breaking the marital bond. With the enactment of no-fault divorce laws, divorce could be granted even though neither party had committed a "fault." With the coming of no-fault divorce it was enough to convince the court that the marriage had broken down, that "irreconcilable differences" existed between the two spouses. In most instances, practically speaking, this was divorce by mutual consent; the two parties had come to an agreement that they wished to go their separate ways, and the court gave ratification to this agreement. But the consent did not need to be *mutual.* If one spouse wished to try to repair the marriage but the other party said, "I am done, and I will never go back"—well, that alone showed the court that the differences truly were irreconcilable. No-fault divorce meant that a marriage, legally speaking, was a very unstable thing; it could be dissolved at the choice, indeed at the whim, of either party. Of course not many marriages are in fact dissolved in a whimsical way, but legally speaking they *can* be. In the USA today and for the last fifty years or so, marriages can be legally dissolved almost as easily as a cube of sugar can be dissolved in a cup of hot tea.

I do not wish to be misunderstood. I am not arguing that the Reformation Protestant belief that Jesus had allowed for an adultery exception to his no-divorce rule had led in a straight line to no-fault divorce. That did not happen. It was the farthest thing in the world from the minds of Luther, Calvin, etc. that the adultery exception should lead to no-fault divorce. It took a long, long time. Over a period of 450 years (from 1517 to 1967) there were many factors—social, cultural, political, military, and economic, combined with this understanding (or rather, misunderstanding) of the teaching of Jesus—that led to no-fault divorce. But this misunderstanding, this incorrect reading of Matthew 5:32 and 19:9, though it may not have been a *sufficient* condition for turning an indissoluble relationship into an easily dissoluble one, was certainly a *necessary* condition. The Reformation attack on the permanence of marriage did not all by itself bring us to our present pass, but the Reformation attack was a great turning point in the history of marriage and family.

10

The Principle of Private Judgment

One other factor needs to be kept in mind when thinking about the Protestant sexual revolution, namely, the great Protestant principle of private judgment.

The Protestant Reformation, whatever else it may have been (and it was many things), was an anti-papal revolution. Protestantism did away with the papacy. The new religion would have no papal monarch sitting at its head. It would have no supreme authority on Earth. Or to phrase this as the Reformers themselves would have phrased it: "The only head of the Church is Jesus Christ, not the pope of Rome who claims—falsely—to be the vicar of Christ; and our only supreme authority is the Bible, the whole Bible, and nothing but the Bible."

But this left Protestants with a difficulty, a difficulty that Catholic apologists did not hesitate to press home. All Protestants (and almost from the very beginning there were many varieties of Protestantism) agreed that the Bible is the supreme authority in religion. But let us suppose two Protestants happen to disagree as to the correct way of interpreting this or that passage of Scripture. Who, there now being no pope, can settle this disagreement? Who can tell the disputants that one of them is right and the other wrong, or that both of them are wrong?

Protestantism could in theory answer that there need be no disagreement. If the two readers were to read the Bible the way it should be read—that is, prayerfully and while asking the Holy Ghost, the true author of the Bible, for guidance in reading it—their interpretations will not disagree; they will understand the Bible passage, thanks to the guidance of the Holy Ghost, in the same way—just as two arithmeticians, if they do their sums correctly, will arrive at the same number. But that answer, while interesting in theory, was no help in practice. In actual practice, as the history of Protestantism has more than amply illustrated, there will be many, many disagreements, even among people who ask the guidance of the Holy Ghost. And since there is no pope or any other ultimate authority on what the Bible says, Protestantism was forced to conclude that every man and every woman would have to decide for himself/herself what this or that Biblical passage really meant. In other words, they would have to use their *private judgment*. Of course they could, and indeed they should, seek advice from their pastor and from learned commentators. But in the last analysis it would have to be the private judgment of every individual Protestant that would decide what the Bible says. From which it followed that the Bible would say a thousand different things to a thousand different people.

Catholics, needless to say, ridiculed all this by saying that the Protestant idea of private judgment was equivalent to saying this: "Every man his own pope."

If you were a Catholic living in the 1500s or 1600s, and you were trying to predict the long-term future of Protestantism, you might well have said something like this: "Given this principle of private judgment, the principle that everyman is his own pope, Protestantism will never be a unified thing. It will break up into fragments; and then the fragments will break up into even smaller fragments; and so on and so forth until finally every Protestant will have his own personal religion."

Well, if you had made this prediction you would have been at least half right. Protestantism, which was never, not even in its sixteenth-century beginnings, a single unified organization, has over the last five hundred years fragmented into a great multitude of churches, denominations, sects, cults, and conventicles. In the United States alone there are hundreds of these, and new ones are appearing or disappearing almost every day.

Present-day Protestants are divided into two groups: liberal or modernist Protestants and conservative or traditional Protestants (these latter usually calling themselves Evangelicals). As for "liberal" Protestants—many of whom are connected with a particular church even though they may not fully subscribe to the official doctrines of that church, and many of whom have no denominational affiliation whatsoever—they pretty much fulfill the prediction that every Protestant will have his own personal religion. By a "liberal" Protestant I mean a Protestant who, as a result of "thinking for himself" about the Bible and religion and morality, has discarded many orthodox or traditional Christian beliefs. It is not rare for one of today's liberal Protestants to have rejected almost all of the articles of the Apostles Creed and the Nicene Creed and to disbelieve in the old commandments against fornication, abortion, and homosexuality. However, it is difficult to find any two liberal Protestants who agree completely in their religious beliefs. And if they agree today, that is no guarantee that they will agree tomorrow, for overnight one or both of them may have had a change of mind about something that was believed today. Every liberal Protestant is what was predicted centuries ago—his or her own pope.

The only things all (or almost all) liberal Protestants agree on are these:

- that Jesus was a good man and a wise moralist, but he was almost certainly not God;
- that something we may call God exists, even though we know little or nothing regarding the nature of this "God";
- that the Bible is a book we should speak of with respect and feel free to quote whenever we can find a passage that supports our religiously liberal opinions—even though the Bible is far from being what Protestantism traditionally considered it to be, the infallible word of God. Alas, it is not that. No, it is a purely man-made book, abounding in historical, philosophical, and moral errors; but it also has some lovely stories and some fine poetry and a great deal of moral wisdom, especially in its New Testament.

However, and perhaps somewhat surprisingly, this career of ever-increasing fragmentation was not followed by *all* Protestants. Over five centuries many of them, traditional or old-fashioned Protestants we may call them, adhered, and continue to adhere even today, to the fundamental Christian dogmas contained in the Nicene Creed. While hardly any Protestant accepts the Nicene Creed as *per se* authoritative, since from the Protestant point of view only the Bible is authoritative, nonetheless traditional Protestants agree with the content of the Nicene Creed; they see the Creed as a handy summary of basic Christian truths. Further, these traditional Protestants have always accepted the ancient Christian code of morality, including sexual morality (except for the Catholic ideal of lifelong celibacy); and thus they hold that the following behaviors are sinful: fornication, masturbation, adultery, pornography, abortion, and homosexual practice. In accepting both the content of the Nicene Creed and the ancient Christian code of morality, these traditional Protestants have been in agreement with Luther, Calvin, and almost all of the early Reformers; moreover, they have been in agreement on these points with Catholics. Both they and Catholics share a belief in what C. S. Lewis called "mere Christianity."[1]

Where can such traditional Protestantism be found in the USA today? Almost exclusively among Protestants who call themselves Evangelicals. While even the Evangelicals have succumbed to the tendency toward organizational fragmentation that is inherent in the Protestant principle of private judgment, they have resisted, for the most part successfully, something else that is commonly associated with that principle, namely the tendency to reject any and all Christian teachings that do not accord with currently fashionable secular beliefs. Rather, they believe in the doctrines expressed in the Nicene Creed, and they believe in the ancient rules of Christian morality (although, needless to say, they do not always obey these rules any more than Catholics do). They subscribe to something that may be called the Protestant Consensus.

The principle of private judgment has brought a mixture of good things and bad things into the world. The principle led, es-

---

[1] See Lewis's book by that name. This book was written during World War II, that is, in the days when Catholics and Protestants held much more in common in the way of Christian beliefs than they do today. The ever-increasing liberalism of liberal Protestantism has largely demolished the old pan-Christian consensus.

pecially among Puritans, the most thoroughly Protestant of all Protestants, to the ideal of universal literacy. If everybody was to judge the Bible for himself or herself, everybody would have to read the Bible; and if everybody was to read the Bible, everybody would first of all have to be able to read. Universal literacy would be needed, and primary schools would be needed to teach that literacy.

The principle led, at least among earnest Protestants, to a great amount of Bible-reading and Bible-study, far more than has ever been found among ordinary Catholics. And if the Bible is a book (or rather, a systematically connected collection of books) whose ultimate author is, as both Catholics and old-fashioned Protestants believe, God the Holy Spirit, then it is a good thing for people to read this God-authored book, even though some of its readers may read it incorrectly.

Over the centuries the principle of private judgment has had a tendency in Protestant countries (for example, the USA) to expand its field of operation, until at last it has led to the common belief that every man and woman has the right to "think for himself"—not just about this or that Biblical passage, but about the Bible as a whole, and about religion generally, and about morality generally, and about everything under the sun—including medical science, as we have seen when it comes to anti-COVID vaccinations.

The modern secular ideal of "thinking for oneself" is no longer confined to Protestant countries, but it had its origin in the Protestant principle of private judgment.

This ideal of free thinking is of course magnificent in some ways; for example, when it allows a fine scientist or scholar to overthrow imperfect conventional wisdom and move on to a higher truth. We are pleased, for example, that Newton and Einstein were able to think for themselves. But it is not so magnificent when it allows a fool to reject genuine wisdom in order to embrace some idiotic moral, intellectual, or aesthetic fashion of the day. Many of our contemporaries do precisely that.

Our present-day world overflows with bad morals, bad ideas, bad manners, and bad music thanks to people who believe themselves to be marvelously open-minded and broad-minded; that is, people who "think for themselves."

But bad ideas are probably the price we have to pay for good ideas. Freedom of thought will lead to good ideas, true; but it is also sure to lead to bad ideas. Thomas Jefferson thought for himself, but so did Adolph Hitler. In any case, the right to think for oneself, a byproduct of the principle of private judgment, was an indispensable condition for three momentous developments: (a) the transition from old-fashioned Protestantism to liberal Protestantism; (b) the later transition from liberal Protestantism to modern atheism; and (c) the moral transition from the Protestant sexual revolution to the modern atheistic sexual revolution.

In summary, the Protestant sexual revolution that began in the 1500s made no attempt to remove all sexual restrictions. Far from it. It got rid of the old Catholic ideal of hyper-chastity, but it retained the Catholic secondary ideal of chastity for ordinary people. What had been the lower ideal of chastity for lay Catholics now became the one and only ideal for Protestantism. And so, while Protestantism had no use for monks or nuns or celibate priests, it held that all Christians must be chaste; that is, must confine sexual activity to intercourse between husband and wife.

Part III

The Modern Sexual Revolution

In this part of the book—the third, the longest, and the final part—I will be discussing the great modern sexual revolution that took place in the United States beginning in the 1960s and is still in progress today. In the early 1960s this latest revolution gave an ethical green light to fornication (premarital sex). In the intervening decades it has expanded its scope, giving its approval to unmarried motherhood, abortion, homosexuality, same-sex marriage, and (most recently) transgenderism. This modern revolution has moved, and is still moving, in the direction of nearly unlimited sexual freedom of action and unlimited freedom of gender identity.

When I say this has been an *atheistic* revolution I don't mean to say that everybody who has approved of this revolution, or who has participated in it, has been an atheist. Not at all. I have two things in mind.

First of all, just as the Protestant sexual revolution of the 1600s was an anti-Catholicism revolution, so this modern sexual revolution has been an anti-Christianity revolution. By endorsing sexual behavior that traditional Christianity, both Catholic and Protestant, has always condemned, the modern revolution is asserting that Christian sexual morality is and always has been wrong. Traditional Protestant sexual morality has been wrong, while traditional Catholic sexual morality has been even worse. And if Christian sexual morality, which has certainly been no small part of Christianity, is wrong, then so is Christianity wrong as a whole; it is a false religion that teaches a defective morality; worse, it is a pernicious religion. But if you're out to destroy Christianity, the most thoroughgoing way of rejecting Christianity is to embrace and promote atheism. What is the first article of the Christian Creed? "I believe in God." Reject God, and the whole Creed collapses. If God doesn't exist, Christianity makes no sense. There can be milder forms of anti-Christianity, but atheism is the most radical and thoroughgoing form.

Second, it is not full-fledged atheists, and full-fledged atheists alone, who are out to destroy Christianity. These full-fledged atheists are the leaders of a coalition of anti-Christianity forces, a coalition that includes a number of semi-atheistic groups, most notably agnostics, religiously indifferent persons, and liberal Protestants (plus liberal Jews[1]). These other groups follow the lead of the atheists in the anti-Christianity struggle. The full-fledged atheists provide the ideas; these others go along with most of these ideas. Since atheists lead this coalition and inspire its non-atheistic members, it is, it seems to me, fair to call it an atheistic coalition. And so, when I call the modern sexual revolution an atheistic revolution, I mean that it is led by atheists and inspired by atheistic ideas.

[1] American Jews are for the most part divided into four categories: Orthodox, Conservative, Reform, and secular (or non-religious). Except for the Orthodox, all the others are either semi-atheistic or frankly atheistic. In other words, except for the Orthodox (a relatively small fraction of the whole), American Jews are religiously liberal (that is, semi-atheistic) or agnostic or fully atheistic.

11

Forerunners of the Modern Revolution

The sexual revolution that took place in the United States[1] beginning in the 1960s happened very suddenly. Almost overnight, it seemed, age-old Christian rules about sexual conduct, rules that both Catholics and Protestants agreed on, were tossed out the window by a generation of young people born after World War II, the so-called "baby boom" generation. All of a sudden fornication was widely considered to be morally okay (provided one took precautions against disease and unwanted pregnancy); and soon thereafter, so was a certain degree of promiscuity; and so was unmarried cohabitation; and so was abortion; and so was divorce even for the lightest of reasons. It took a bit longer for homosexuality to win the popular seal of approval; but eventually—and quite logically, given the principle of sexual freedom that had been embraced by the baby boom generation—it did.

To this day adultery has *not* won widespread approval. It seems odd, however, that it should still be so generally disapproved of. Given the widely accepted rule that sexual acts are morally okay provided they are done between two consenting adults, what objection can there be to voluntary adultery? (Perhaps in that case we need *three* consenting adults: lover #1, lover #2, and the "innocent" spouse who will say, "Please don't mind me; I have no objec-

---

[1] And in the Western world generally. Despite this, I will focus on the sexual revolution as it took place in the United States, and this for two reasons. For one, I am an American, and am therefore much better acquainted with the sexual revolution as it happened (and is still happening) in the United States than in other countries. Second, I am writing this book with a readership in mind that will be chiefly American.

tion.") Neither has polygamy—or its virtual equivalent, polyamory—won anything like majority approval. This seems very odd indeed. For if same-sex marriage (a new thing in the history of the world) has won general approval, which it has if we are to judge from public opinion surveys, why should polygamy (an ancient and, for much of human history, a greatly honored institution) be thought badly of? My hunch is that with time the logic of the ongoing sexual revolution will work its magic, and that adultery, polygamy, and polyamory *will* win widespread public acceptance. That is not to say that great numbers of people will actually engage in adultery or polygamy/polyamory. There are many activities we approve of without *doing* them. For instance, almost everybody approves of water polo even though hardly anybody plays it. Likewise there is general approval of homosexual activity even though only a small fraction of the population engages in such activity. In the foreseeable future, then, I expect that if the sexual revolution continues on its present track we will soon see widespread approval of, though perhaps not the practice of, adultery, polygamy, and polyandry.

Although the full-fledged sexual revolution arrived suddenly in the United States in the 1960s, it did not come as a bolt from the blue. It had forerunners earlier in the twentieth century, individuals or institutions or events that prepared the ground for what was to come. At least eight of these are worth mentioning.

(1) Feminism. If feminism is defined as a movement demanding that women have legal, social, and political equality with men, then we can say that there were rumblings of feminism in the Anglo-American world as early as the late eighteenth century; see Mary Wollstonecraft's book *A Vindication of the Rights of Women* (1792).[2] It became a minor but significant movement in the USA in the middle years of the nineteenth century; in 1848 a famous "rights of women" convention was held at Seneca Falls NY. But it was not until the early twentieth century that the movement became a powerful cultural force. During the first two decades of

[2] The book was reprinted in 1992 by Dover Publications. The author, an Englishwoman, was the wife of the political philosopher and novelist William Godwin, and was also the mother of Mary Shelley, author of *Frankenstein*.

the century its great goal was winning the right to vote, which was finally accomplished in 1920 thanks to the Nineteenth Amendment to the US Constitution.

During the 1920s (the "roaring twenties"), in the aftermath of both the Nineteenth Amendment and World War I, typical unmarried young women of the middle classes became noticeably more "free" than ever before. They wore short skirts (quite unlike the ankle-length skirts that had been mandatory prior to the war), they smoked cigarettes, they drank alcohol in public, and they spent, thanks especially to that relatively new thing, the automobile, much greater amounts of un-chaperoned time with young men. During World War II many women ("Rosie the riveter") did jobs hitherto done by men, who were now unavailable because of military service. Naturally this gave such women greater feelings of independence and self-reliance, and these feelings did not totally disappear after the war.

In the 1960s a renewed feminist movement appeared on the national scene; it can be dated from the appearance in 1963 of Betty Friedan's landmark book, *The Feminine Mystique*. At first this new feminism's great demand was for equality with men in the workplace, but it very soon added to its demands a demand for sexual equality. In theory this might have been a demand that men be held to the strict sexual standards that had heretofore been applied to women. But in practice it became a demand that women be allowed the sexual freedom that had been allowed to men; a demand to do away with the age-old "double standard" in sexual morality. Soon there was a great expansion of the sexual freedom that was allowed to both women and men (the sexual revolution). Soon, too, there was a great demand for abortion rights. And logically so; for how can a society adopt a moral regime of great sexual freedom if it does not back up this freedom with a right to abortion when things go wrong? A few years later (1973) the US Supreme Court gave its support to the sexual revolution with its *Roe v. Wade* ruling, according to which the US Constitution contains an implied right to abortion.

(2) Hollywood. If we say that a movie qualifies for the description "explicitly sexual" only if it presents a scene with characters engaging in an act of sexual intercourse, we may say that movies were not explicitly sexual until the 1960s. But they were implicitly sexual long before that, going back to the era of silent films. How was this done? How did Hollywood suggest a sexual act without actually showing it? By making it clear (except perhaps to children in the audience) that the romantic relationship between two unmarried characters in the film involved sexual intercourse. Sometimes this clarity was achieved by broad hints. At other times it was achieved by showing almost everything but the act itself. For instance, in a dark room late at night the two lovers hug and kiss and whisper words of love; then comes a fade-to-black; next we see them at breakfast the following morning.

More influential perhaps than the movies themselves were the sexually scandalous lives of glamorous movie stars, many of whom married-and-divorced-and-remarried two or three or more times. And although studio publicists pretended that these frequently-wed stars were chaste during the interval between marriages, everybody (again, except for children) knew this was not the case. Those who admiringly followed the lives of glamorous stars were both shocked and pleased to realize that many of these stars were living sexually liberated lives. Hollywood, these fans imagined, was something of a sexual paradise. And by following the lives of these stars, fans (especially female fans) were able to pay vicarious visits to this paradise.

(3) Bertrand Russell. Russell (1872–1970) was one of the leading English philosophers of the twentieth century, specializing in logic, epistemology, the philosophy of science, the philosophy of mathematics, and the history of philosophy.[3] However, in addition to his strictly philosophical works, he wrote many "popular" books on such topics as politics, economics, psychology, sociology, education, ethics, political-social history, religion (or anti-religion, for Russell was an atheist who deplored religion, Christianity in particular), and sex. He also wrote a three-volume autobiography. He wrote incidentally about sexual morality (or

[3] See his big fat book, *A History of Western Philosophy* (first published in 1945, still in print today). This is a very readable, entertaining, and informative book, significantly marred however by Russell's anti-religion prejudices.

immorality) in many books, but especially in his 1929 book *Marriage and Morals*. In 1950 he was awarded the Nobel Prize for Literature.

Russell himself made a sharp distinction between his two kinds of writing, philosophical and popular; he made it clear that he did not write the latter in his capacity as philosopher. But much of his reading audience did not bother to make this distinction. They considered all his writings to be philosophical, and since a philosopher is supposed to be a wise man, much of the public took his popular books to be books abounding in wisdom. Given this philosophical prestige and given the fact that Russell's popular writings were fluent and often very witty, he was widely read and had considerable influence on public opinion, especially in Britain and the USA.

His books sold well in the USA, at least in part because of his quite explicit anti-Christianity. At the time it was considered bad form in America to write against Christianity and in support of atheism. America's most famous philosophical atheist, John Dewey (1859–1952), was not explicit about his atheism; you had to find it by reading between his lines—his rather tedious lines, I may add; he was as dull a writer as Russell was lively. So if you were an American and you wanted a reputable thinker who expressed your anti-Christian and anti-theistic sentiments, you were likely to turn to Russell, who was writing his anti-Christian and anti-theistic opinions on the other side of the Atlantic Ocean.

In *Marriage and Morals*, Russell (who himself had sex relationships with many women, including his four wives; three of his marriages ended in divorce) defended what was in that day (1929) a very "advanced" sex ethic. Today his "advanced" ethic would be rather a conventional sex ethic among liberal persons. He gave his approval to sexual equality between men and women (that is, whatever sexual freedom society allows to men should also be allowed to women); to premarital sex; to "trial marriages" (that is, unmarried cohabitation); to "easy" divorce. And to adultery in some circumstances. These circumstances included a relatively prolonged separation of husband and wife; Russell once suggested that a three-week separation would justify adultery, though only with the consent of the other spouse.

In 1941 Russell was given an appointment as professor of philosophy at the City College of New York (CCNY), an appointment that was scheduled to last from February 1, 1941, to June 30, 1942. He was scheduled to teach three courses having to do with logic, mathematics, science, and metaphysics. His courses would not deal with morality or religion or sex. Nonetheless a storm of public protest arose, initiated by William Thomas Manning (1866–1949), the Episcopal[4] bishop of New York City (1921–46), who wrote to New York newspapers denouncing the appointment of "a man who is a recognized propagandist against both religion and morality, and who specifically defends adultery." This triggered a widespread attack on the Russell appointment by newspapers, politicians (many of them Irish Catholics), patriotic organizations, and religious organizations (many of these Catholic). The controversy took on a national dimension as many distinguished figures from the academic world rallied to Russell's support. This list of supporters included such intellectual luminaries as Robert Hutchins, Curt Ducasse, Arthur Lovejoy, Carl Becker, Alfred North Whitehead, John Dewey, Albert Einstein, Sidney Hook, Morris Raphael Cohen, and John Herman Randall. These supporters were not defending Russell's opinions about sex; they were simply defending his freedom to teach and his right of free speech.

A taxpayer, the parent of a City College student, went to court asking that Russell's appointment be annulled. Her lawyer described Russell's writings as "lecherous, libidinous, lustful, venereous, erotomaniac, aphrodisiac, irreverent, narrow-minded, untruthful, and bereft of moral fiber." The judge ruled against Russell, revoking his appointment to CCNY, basing his ruling on "the laws of nature and of nature's God." The hiring of Russell, the judge said, was "in effect establishing a chair of indecency." The City of New York could have appealed the judge's ruling to a higher court, but the city (whose mayor at the time was Fiorello

[4] In those days the Episcopal Church in the USA had not become what it is today, a liberal church.

LaGuardia) decided not to appeal. Russell never got to teach at City College.[5]

Although Russell lost the legal battle in a courtroom, he won in the more important court of public opinion—or perhaps I should say, in the court of *educated* public opinion. In this more important court the foes (especially the many Catholic foes) of Russell looked foolish. For one thing, their campaign against Russell showed that they did not appreciate the value and importance of academic freedom and free speech. Second, they seemed to imagine that a professor lecturing on such dry subjects as mathematics and epistemology could somehow corrupt the sexual morals of his student audience. Finally, their real motive for blocking Russell was not a genuine fear that he would corrupt the morals of CCNY students; rather, it was an attempt to injure and insult a man who was a notorious freethinker on questions of religion and morality. In sum, they hurt themselves more than they hurt Russell, and in hurting themselves they did damage to the religion and the sexual morality they claimed to be defending. For with friends like these, who needs enemies? In their ill-advised campaign against Russell they helped Russell in his long campaign against Christianity and its sexual morality.

(4) Margaret Sanger. Sanger (1879–1966) is often called "the mother of birth control" in America. Her parents were both immigrants from Ireland, her father an atheist, her mother a Catholic. Her mother was pregnant eighteen times and gave birth eleven times, Margaret being the sixth of these eleven children. Margaret and her first husband, William Sanger, moved to New York City in 1911, where she worked as a visiting nurse in the slums of the Lower East Side of Manhattan. She and her husband became involved in the radical politics of Greenwich Village bohemians. The couple separated in 1913 and were officially divorced in 1921. The next year she married her second husband, James Slee.

In 1914 she was indicted for violating postal obscenity laws by sending literature promoting contraception through the mails.

---

[5] This account of the CCNY case I have taken from the Appendix to the Russell book, *Why I Am not a Christian*, edited by the philosopher Paul Edwards (1957), pages 207-59. Edwards is the author of the Appendix.

Rather than stand trial, she fled to Europe, where she met and interacted with well-known proponents of contraception and sexual liberation, including Havelock Ellis. Returning to the United States, in 1916 she opened America's first legal birth control clinic in Brooklyn. She founded the American Birth Control League in 1921, which in 1942 changed its name to the Planned Parenthood Federation of America.

In those days Planned Parenthood was not what it is now, a great provider of abortion. In fact it was not an abortion provider at all; it was a provider of contraception. Margaret Sanger died a few years before the Supreme Court's *Roe v. Wade* ruling of 1973 made abortion on demand a constitutionally protected right, after which Planned Parenthood got into the abortion business in a big way; so it is not perfectly clear what Sanger would have thought about her agency's becoming the nation's number one abortion provider. From the beginning of her birth control career she had routinely argued that contraception was a way of preventing the need for abortion. But given that she had been since early in the twentieth century a supporter of the idea that women should be sexually free and the further idea that women should not have to bear children against their will, it is very likely, indeed it is almost certain, that she would have approved of, indeed rejoiced at, Planned Parenthood's turn to abortion.

From the teen years of the twentieth century forward, Margaret Sanger was America's most well-known champion of contraception. At the beginning of her birth control crusade, she faced tremendous opposition. The opposition came from churches, both Catholic and Protestant, and even from government authorities. But she gradually won her way. Government authorities soon lost interest in prosecuting her or any others who operated birth control clinics or spread pro-contraception propaganda. In the period between the two World Wars Protestant churches became increasingly tolerant of the use of contraception by married couples. A critical moment in this evolution came in 1930, when at its Lambeth Conference (held in London) the worldwide Anglican Communion (including the American Episcopal Church) endorsed the use of contraception by married couples in certain circumstances. But of course once contraception was widely practiced among married couples, there was, practically speaking, little likelihood that this practice would not widely spread among unmarried couples.

The Catholic Church held out for a long time, continuing to oppose contraception, including especially marital contraception,[6] into the 1960s, after the sexual revolution was well underway. In 1968 there was great expectation among "progressive" Catholics that Pope Paul VI was on the verge of announcing that the Church had changed its mind on contraception; for a study commission had made such a recommendation to the pope. And then in the middle of the year the Pope made his announcement—and it was just the opposite of what progressives had hoped for. In his encyclical *Humanae Vitae* Pope Paul, so far from giving the green light to contraception, reaffirmed in no uncertain terms the traditional red light. Marital contraception, the Pope said, is a great sin, and he gave reasons for reiterating the traditional ban. This sparked an in-house rebellion not just among Catholic laity but among many priests as well. Hundreds of Catholic theologians, most of them priests, took out a full-page ad in the New York Times announcing their dissent from the encyclical. Bishops generally supported the pope, or at least did not publicly dissent. Many parish priests, however, privately advised their parishioners that they should "follow their conscience"—which, translated into plain English, meant, "If you think that contraception is right for you, go ahead and practice contraception, and disregard not just Pope Paul VI but the age-old teaching of the Church."

After that, for all practical purposes, Catholic opposition to contraception collapsed. To be sure, the Church officially adheres to the present day to what Pope Paul VI said; it still teaches that contraception is a serious sin; and it promotes a kind of birth control that it calls "natural family planning"—a kind of periodic

[6] It is not quite clear what the Catholic position is regarding the use of contraception during acts of fornication or adultery. Does contraception (a) mitigate the evils of fornication and adultery by removing, or at least greatly reducing, the risk of unmarried pregnancy? Or does it (b) aggravate the sins of fornication and adultery by adding to them the further sin of contraception?

abstention that has mockingly been called "Vatican roulette." But most American Catholics disagree, and most Catholic married couples have at some time or other in their marriages practiced contraception, and it is likely that young unmarried American Catholics use contraception while fornicating or cohabiting at about the same rate as non-Catholic unmarried couples. It is a rare parish priest who preaches against contraception from the pulpit at weekend Masses. For that matter it is a rare parish priest who speaks from the pulpit against any sexual sins, including homosexuality. A visitor from Mars who randomly attended Catholic churches for a year, and listened to priestly homilies, would have no clue that Catholicism is a religion that officially teaches that contraception, fornication, adultery, homosexual conduct, and abortion are sinful; and not just sinful, but sinful in a very serious way.

To be sure, there are holdouts here and there. There are Catholic couples who strictly abstain from contraception; and these are often the finest young couples in the Church. There are still many priests, especially younger priests, who, even when privately counseling parishioners, are quite willing to defend the *Humanae Vitae* teaching. There are some brave priests who sermonize against abortion; and there are some super-brave priests who sermonized against homosexual conduct.

Yet for the most part Margaret Sanger has won, even among Catholics. And of course, once society has endorsed marital contraception it has put its foot on a long and slippery slope that leads to abortion. The endorsement of marital contraception leads more or less logically to the endorsement of nonmarital contraception; at least it does so in a society which, like Western societies today, has given the okay to a high level of sexual freedom. And the endorsement of nonmarital sex and contraception leads logically to an endorsement of abortion. For contraception does not always work, and when it does not it is necessary to have a failsafe arrangement at hand; otherwise how can you have a regime of sexual freedom? Needless to say, we Americans did not slide all the way down the slippery slope overnight. It took decades. It has happened slowly—but it has happened surely.

(5) Sigmund Freud. For decades Freud, the great Viennese psychologist, psychiatrist, and founder of psychoanalysis, was taken by most of his American fans to be a champion of sexual liberation. We must keep in mind, however, that the vast majority of his American "fans" were not professional psychologists or psychiatrists. No, they were more or less educated lay persons. They were men and women (sometimes little more than boys and girls) who had heard about Freud in a college classroom or in an informal conversation, or had read about him in a book or in magazine articles, or had read something (not very much) written by Freud himself.

The idea that he was a champion of sexual liberation was an error—or at least it was a tremendous exaggeration. While Freud was opposed to what he would consider to be excessive sexual repression—the repression, for instance, experienced by many middle-class Viennese women who were his patients, and experienced by many middle-class Victorian women generally, not just the women of Vienna—he was far from a foe of sexual repression generally.

In his small book *Civilization and Its Discontents*, Freud made it clear that a significant degree of sexual repression is necessary for civilization. We cannot maximize *both* sexual liberation *and* civilization. One of the great prices men and women have had to pay for the advances of civilization is a restraint on sexual desires. We can have unlimited sexual freedom, or we can have civilization. We cannot have both.

Would we like to give ourselves over to lives of unmitigated pleasure? At some irrational level of our being, Freud says, that is precisely what we would like, but at a more rational level we know that this is impossible. We are guided by both a pleasure principle and a reality principle; and often they are in conflict with one another. And so we prefer civilization despite the frustrations and sometimes the miseries that are the price we have to pay for it. For some people the price is excessively high, and they slip into one or another kind of mental illness. Most of us, however, limp on, living lives that are a mix of happiness and unhappiness, getting some pleasure out of life, but not nearly as much as we would like.

Some American fans of Freud, those who had actually taken the trouble to read him carefully, understood that he was saying this. They understood that he was not a champion of fully liberated sexuality; far from it. But other fans, those whose understanding of Freud was based more on wishful thinking than on careful study, did not understand. They had the impression, a false impression, that he was calling for nearly unrestricted sexual freedom. They had the impression that he was saying that such freedom would bring not only robust mental health but positive happiness in life.

It is not strange that, in an era (the pre-1960s era) when the United States did not have a cultural regime of sexual freedom, those who yearned for such a regime would wish to find some eminent figure who could serve as a great symbolic champion of such freedom. So they found Freud, the world's most famous psychologist and most famous sexologist. That they had to misunderstand him to elevate him to this championship position was a small price to pay. But when the real thing arrived, that is, when the sexual revolution of the '60s introduced a genuine culture of sexual freedom to the USA, Freud was no longer needed, and so he soon lost his position of great popular eminence.

It should be noted, however, that two other factors, both of them aspects of the sexual revolution, contributed to his fall. One was the feminist movement. There was, and still is, much more to feminism that sexual liberation; but almost from the beginning sexual freedom for women (and girls) has been an essential element of the feminist agenda. Feminists have been deeply offended by Freud's theory that girls and women suffer from "penis envy," a theory they regard as both nonsensical and profoundly sexist. Freud had to go.

The other factor was the gay/lesbian rights movement, later subsumed into the broader LGBTQ+ movement. Freud had taught that homosexuality is the result of arrested sexual development. One's sexuality develops in stages, and the highest stage, the fully mature stage, is heterosexual genital sexuality. "Normal" women, that is, women who have arrived at this highest stage, desire sexual intercourse with men, not with other women; and "normal" men, that is, men who have arrived at this highest stage, desire sexual intercourse with women, not with other men. Needless to say, this theory was intolerable to persons active in the gay/lesbian rights movement. Freud had to go.

Poor Freud! He had been immensely popular for reasons that had little to do with his scientific merits, and he was later rejected for reasons that had little to do with any lack of scientific merits.

(6) Margaret Mead. Margaret Mead (1901–78) wrote a famous book that made a considerable contribution to the idea that sexual freedom is a good thing. The book, first published in 1928, is titled *Coming of Age in Samoa*. It was an anthropological best-seller. It was especially widely read by college students in the twenty years or so between the end of World War II and the middle 1960s. These were the decades when, thanks largely to the GI Bill of Rights, there was an explosion in the percentage of high school graduates who went on to college. It was the period when college-going, instead of being a rare thing done by young men and young women of America's more privileged social classes, became more or less "normal" for Americans of all but the very lowest classes.[7] Professors of anthropology or sociology often made *Coming of Age in Samoa* required reading. It was easy to read and fun to read while at the same time being an intellectually serious book—just the kind of thing a professor would be happy to assign to his students.

Mead belonged to the Cultural Relativism school of anthropology, the leader of which was her teacher at Columbia, Franz Boas. In the first half of the twentieth century this school replaced the Cultural Evolution school as the leading school of anthropology.[8]

---

[7] It was in the 1960s that an attempt to make college available to even the lowest classes led to a tremendous expansion of public 2-year colleges (usually called community colleges), colleges marked by open enrollment and inexpensive tuition fees. Further attempts along this line are being made today by politicians who call for free tuition at 2-year colleges or even free tuition at 4-year public colleges.

[8] Another famous member of this school was Ruth Benedict (1887–1948), also a student of Boas at Columbia. Benedict, like Mead, wrote a best-selling book that professors of sociology and/or anthropology were in the habit of requiring their students to read, especially during the postwar decades of 1945–

In her twenties Mead went to Samoa, where she spent nine months doing a study of native adolescent girls. It was generally believed in America at the time that adolescence was pretty much the same everywhere in the world in that it was a time of trouble for teens and their parents; a time of "storm and stress" as young people go through the difficult transition from childhood to adulthood. Mead suspected this was not so. In keeping with her general theory of cultural relativism, she suspected that the psychology of the teen years in one culture might differ radically from the psychology of the teen years in another culture. And this suspicion was confirmed by her observations of, and her conversations with, Samoan girls. In Samoa the transition years between childhood and adulthood went much more smoothly than in America. There was far less anxiety and far less conflict between parents and children.

Much of this, Mead surmised, was due to the relaxed attitude Samoans had to premarital teenage sex. Despite the fact that Christianity, thanks to Protestant missionaries, was making inroads among Samoans, Samoan girls and boys still adhered to an older, pre-Christian sexual ethic, a very permissive ethic. According to Mead's informants among the girls, unmarried boys and girls were quite free to have casual sex with one another. This sexual freedom did not give the teens a bad conscience; neither did it provoke parents to anger. Of course parents might object when their daughter slept with this or that *particular* boy; but they had no principled objection to her sleeping with *some* boy (or boys).

There were exceptions, however, to this general rule of sexual permissiveness. For one, girls from socially high-ranking families were expected to be virgins at the moment of their wedding. For another, some non-high-ranking girls who were quite definitely not virgins at their wedding nonetheless *claimed* to be virgins.

And so certain questions as to the accuracy of Mead's report may be asked.

---

65. The title of this once-famous book is *Patterns of Culture* (first published 1934). Benedict and Mead were good friends, and some, including Mead's daughter, believe that for a while they had a lesbian relationship. I myself am not convinced there is sufficient evidence to support this belief.

- If virginity was expected of girls in the "best" families, why did this ideal not "trickle down" to girls in ordinary families?
- If girls from ordinary families were socially permitted to sleep with boys, and did in fact sleep with them, why would some of these girls wish to be thought virgins at the time of their wedding? Why did they not say to their husband and his family, "Of course I'm not a virgin. As we all know, that's what we Samoan girls do; we have premarital sex with boys."
- If boys and girls were freely sleeping with one another, why were there few out-of-wedlock births? Why were almost all brides not conspicuously pregnant at their weddings?
- If Samoan teenagers spent a few premarital years engaging in premarital sex with multiple partners, why didn't this habit carry over into their married years? That is: Why wasn't adultery a common thing among married persons? To be sure, it took place (as it takes place in every society); but, to judge from Mead's book, it was no more common in Samoa than elsewhere in the world.

In 1983 (five years after Mead died) John Derek Freeman, a New Zealand anthropologist, published a book, *Margaret Mead and Samoa: the Making and Unmaking of an Anthropological Myth*, in which he argued that Mead had misunderstood and therefore misreported the situation in Samoa. Freeman had interviewed two of the girls, now old women, who had been Mead's informants more than fifty years earlier, and they told him that they had joked with Mead, telling her stories of sexual adventures that had never taken place.

Freeman argued that in fact, contrary to Mead's belief, Samoans place a high value on chastity and premarital virginity. Freeman's book sparked great controversy in the world of anthropology, for it would be a tremendous scandal if Mead, one of the most famous and most revered figures in that world, had made so colossal a mistake. To this day Mead has her ardent defenders; and to this day other anthropologists agree with Freeman. The anthropological community remains divided.

Regardless of whether or not Mead had been deceived by her Samoan informants, she wrote her famous and influential book believing what the girls had told her—believing that Samoan boys and girls engaged in a great deal of multi-partner premarital sex; that they did this with the approval of their society and their parents; and that they did it with no significant psychological harm to themselves. Though Mead herself was not a Freudian, her book reinforced what many people assumed (erroneously) to be Freud's lesson, namely, that sexual freedom, so far from being a bad thing, is a good thing, a psychologically healthy thing.

College students reading Mead in the postwar decades (1945–65) could hardly avoid drawing the conclusion that it was possible, and even desirable, for society to have a sexual ethic that allowed for more or less casual premarital sex. If it was the actual case in Samoa, why could it not be the case in America—provided we made a small number of cultural adjustments? So let's promote the following cultural changes:

- Let's have an attitude of tolerance. The postwar decades in the USA saw a great and growing increase in racial tolerance. So let's be tolerant in other matters. Let's have a great increase in sexual tolerance. Why should we feel retrospective jealousy at the previous sex partners that our current lover (or spouse) may have had?
- Let's have a great decline of the sexual puritanism associated with Christianity—and perhaps a general decline in Christianity, which has interrupted the legitimate pleasures of the world for too many centuries.
- Let's make the use of contraception a routine thing.
- And in case contraception fails or is neglected, let's legalize abortion.

It was a small step from Mead's portrait of Samoa as a teenage sexual paradise to the American sexual revolution.

(7) The Kinsey Reports. Alfred Kinsey was a professor of zoology at the University of Indiana. In the years not long after World War II he and his associates (Kinsey was the leader of a large research team) published two studies popularly known as the Kinsey Reports. The proper names of these books were: *Sexual Behavior in the Human Male* (1948) and *Sexual Behavior in the Human Female* (1953).

The titles were inaccurate. They should have been titled something like "Sexual behavior in American males and females in the middle years of the twentieth century." For the subjects of the two studies were *American* males and females, not males and females worldwide; and the studies did not range beyond the twentieth century. I suppose this misnaming reflects the fact that Kinsey was a zoologist, not a psychologist or sociologist or historian. If you are a zoologist and you wish to study the sexual behavior of a certain species or subspecies of wild animal, it does not much matter where the animal comes from or in what century it lived; all wild animals of this or that particular kind are pretty much the same. But humans are *cultural* animals, and as cultures differ from one another so do the behaviors of humans living in this or that culture.

Critics found other faults with the Kinsey reports. Some complained that the Americans studied in the reports were not a truly representative sample of Americans. Others complained that the reports reduced the "sexual behavior" it purported to be studying to a number of physical acts of sex, disregarding the emotional and social context in which these acts take place.

In any case, the two reports, though heavily laden with page after page of dry statistics, became best-sellers. And those who did not read the books were able to read brief summaries of their contents in newspapers and magazines. Never had the public been so much interested in a scientific (or should I say "scientific"?) study.

Why were these reports so popular? Because some of the findings in the two Kinsey studies were "sensational"—sensational in that they reported that Americans were engaging in unconventional or immoral sexual behavior far more frequently than almost anybody had imagined. For instance:

- There was more premarital sex than had been popularly supposed.
- There was more adultery than had been popularly supposed.
- There was more homosexuality than had been popularly supposed.
- All these behaviors were on the increase as decades passed, and, it seemed probable, would further increase in the future.

The word "normal" has two very different meanings. On the one hand it means that which is *average*. For instance, in the city of X it is *normal* that the January temperature will be about thirty degrees Fahrenheit; in other words, thirty degrees is the *average* January temperature. Or in the same city it is normal that twenty murders will be committed *per annum*; in other words, twenty is the *average* number of murders.

On the other hand, "normal" sometimes means that which conforms to an ideal standard; that which is as it should be. And so it is normal for a police officer to abstain from committing crime, and it is normal for a teacher to grade students on the basis of merit. Likewise it is normal for a husband or wife to have sexual relations with nobody but his or her spouse, and it is normal for the judge at a trial to remain impartial as between the two parties.

It is easy to confuse these two meanings—just as it is easy to confuse the two meanings of an almost synonymous word, "natural." Something can be natural in the sense of "usual" or natural in the sense of "as it should be."

The Kinsey reports confused (or confounded or conflated) the double meanings of "normal" and "natural," asserting in effect that behavior that is usual is also behavior as it should be. Thus a certain amount of fornication is right because it is usual, and a certain amount of adultery is right because it is usual, and a certain amount of homosexuality is right because it is usual. It seems clear that Kinsey and his team committed this equivocation more or less intentionally (though no doubt a certain amount of stupidity contributed). The aim of the team, it seems clear, was not just to report on American sexuality, but to loosen it up; to encourage tolerance of much of what had hitherto been considered sexual deviance, and thus to move much sexual behavior from the category of "deviant" to the category of "non-deviant."

A variety of public reactions followed publication of these famous reports.

- Many strong believers in traditional sexual morality, instead of saying, "This is bad news; let us embark on a purity crusade," said instead, "This is false; it is defective science; it is a libel against the overwhelmingly chaste American public."

- Other traditionalists said, "Well, I do not like this, but I have to accept the fact that I am living in a very naughty world. So be it. I have to put up with other things I do not like and cannot change, for example, political corruption and bad weather. So I will put up with this too."
- Others said: "I used to think I was a great sexual sinner. I see now that I am about average. I see there is no need for me to have a guilty conscience."
- Still others said: "I thought my restrained sex conduct was normal, much like that of my neighbors. I see now that I have been lagging behind. My neighbors have been having more fun, more adventure. It is time for me to catch up with others, time to commit what I used to think of as sexual sins."

The Kinsey Reports contributed to the loosening of the rules of sexual morality—just as earlier contributions had been made by Hollywood, Margaret Sanger, the fans of Sigmund Freud, Bertrand Russell, and Margaret Mead. It was now the 1950s. The stage was now set for the 1960s and the coming of the sexual revolution.

(8) The Pill. During the 1950s a birth control pill was developed, largely at the prompting of Margaret Sanger; and in 1960 the US Food and Drug Administration gave its approval. "The Pill" came on the market and soon proved to be very popular. At first it was touted as a benefit for married couples, allowing them better to "space" their children. It was not promoted as a boon for unmarried persons. But once it was on the market, how, practically speaking, could it be kept away from unmarried women and girls—especially when their boyfriends (and sometimes their mothers) were demanding that they utilize the new pill?

Was the pill an important factor in bringing about the sexual revolution? In my opinion, no, not very much. For the revolution was first of all a revolution in moral *attitudes*; only secondarily a revolution in moral *behavior* that followed from those attitudes. The pill was simply a tool that facilitated that behavior, albeit a very helpful tool. Yet there were other contraceptive tools available prior to the invention of the pill; for example, condoms and diaphragms and IUDs. The pill simply added one more tool to the contraceptive toolkit—for women a user-friendly tool. The time was ripe. The sexual revolution was bound to happen, pill or no pill.

The true significance of the pill in this story, it seems to me, is as a symbol. It appeared on the scene at precisely the moment when the sexual revolution was about to take off. If you are the kind of person who likes being able to give a more or less precise date when this or that historical era begins (I myself happen to be that kind of person), 1960—the year of the pill—is as good a year as any for marking the start of the sexual revolution.

12

The Never-ending Sexual Revolution

When the sexual revolution commenced in the early 1960s, probably not many people guessed that it would still be in progress in the 2020s; that it would still be expanding, still finding new forms of sexual liberation.

The expansion of the sexual revolution came in stages, the later stages following from the earlier in a kind of logical progression. This chapter outlines these stages.

Premarital Sex

When the sexual revolution began, its main concern was to provide moral legitimacy for premarital sex (fornication) between college boys and college girls. Premarital sex between lower-class boys and girls had been taking place forever. Premarital virginity had never been much of a lower-class ideal; however, it *was* an ideal for middle-class people—and, it should be added, for that section of the lower class who had middle-class aspirations. But many lower-class kids (those from the lower half of the lower class) repudiated middle-class values generally, including middle-class sexual values. These kids were well aware of course that chastity was a value believed in by "respectable" people, and that these respectable people would disapprove when these lower-class boys and girls engaged in fornication. But these same respectable people (e.g., schoolteachers, cops, social workers) disapproved of almost everything these lower-class kids did—for instance, their bad language, their delinquent and near-delinquent behavior, their refusal to take school and schoolwork seriously. So why fret about their disapproval of premarital sex?

Lower-class kids, aware that the lower-class way of life was disapproved of by respectable people, reacted in one of three ways. (1) Some lower-class kids took this criticism to heart and made up their minds that they would do the right thing and eventually become respectable themselves. (2) Others concluded that it was their destiny never to become respectable, and so in the meantime they would keep their heads down, stay pretty much out of trouble, and get whatever small satisfactions from life their inferior social positions would allow them. (3) Still others resented this condemnation by respectable people, and quite deliberately rejected these people and their values; they "rejected their rejecters." Many of them became juvenile delinquents, and some of them went on to have criminal careers as adults. As boys, they swore, they lied, they cheated, they stole, they shoplifted, they stole cars to take "joy rides," they vandalized property, they got into fist fights, they mugged people on the streets, and so on. Usually they did all these things as part of a gang, a gang of "bad boys" and a few "bad girls." The respectable world reacted by saying, "How awful"—and this reaction pleased the kids. They were shocking the bourgeoisie, and that was the whole point.[1]

Boys, and to a lesser extent girls, in category #3 rejected middle-class sexual values. Boys and girls (especially girls) in category #1 accepted middle-class sexual values, even if in practice they sometimes deviated from these values. Boys and girls in category #2 were a mixture, not as "good" as category #1 kids, and not nearly as "bad" as category #3 kids.

When college boys and girls began, on a widespread basis, having premarital sex in the 1960s, they were not saying to themselves, "We want to be bad boys and bad girls—just like lower-class kids." Not at all. These college boys and girls had always been, or at least had always aspired to be, good boys and girls; respectable kids; the respectable sons and daughters of respectable parents. They had grown up in respectable neighborhoods; they had been respectable students in high school, and they had

[1] I have borrowed this account of the three lower-class reactions from that sociological classic, *Delinquent Boys*, by Albert Cohen (The Free Press, 1955). However, what I am calling the "lower class" Cohen called the "working class."

gone on to be respectable students at respectable colleges. Now that they were 18 or 19 or 20 or 21, they wanted to have sex. But at the same time they had no wish to be bad; they wanted to remain good; they wanted to remain respectable. And so this first stage of the sexual revolution, what we may call the fornication stage, comprised two elements:

- college students having unmarried sex to a much greater degree than had ever happened among their predecessor generations
- college students declaring that there is nothing wrong with premarital sex provided certain conditions are met, these conditions being two;
  - that there be at least some real affection (love) between the partners;
  - that the couple take "precautions" against pregnancy.

The sexual revolution, in other words, was not just a significant change in sexual *conduct*; more important, it was a very radical change in the *moral evaluation* of sexual conduct. What had hitherto been bad, very seriously bad, now became not just non-bad but positively good. What had been impermissible became, not just permissible, but something close to mandatory. Hitherto it had been wrong of a girl to lose her virginity prior to marriage; henceforth it would be wrong for a girl to *retain* her virginity until marriage.

If you were to tell the rebellious boys and girls of the lower class that it is wrong of them to engage in premarital sex, they would reply: "So what? Who cares?" But if you were to tell these college boys and girls that it is wrong of them to engage in premarital sex, they would reply: "No it isn't. It is okay for us to do this." And they would give you reasons for this.

- "We take precautions against pregnancy."
- "We love one another . . . at least for now."
- "Our sexual encounters cause no harm to anybody."
- "This is part of our maturation process."
- "We owe it to our eventual spouses to be experienced in the ways of love and sex before we marry."
- "This is what nature calls on us to do."

- "In the old days farmers and their wives married at the age of eighteen. Modern city-dwellers postpone marriage. It is unreasonable and unnatural to postpone sex until we are getting close to middle age."
- "Everybody else is doing this, and according to the old proverb, 'When in Rome, do as the Romans do.'"
- "When I marry, I will almost certainly learn that my spouse has not retained his/her virginity. Why should I retain mine?"
- "You [the critic] are old-fashioned, awfully out-of-date."

That was the beginning—fornication or premarital sex. But from that beginning followed a cascade of other sexual or sex-related behaviors that flowed more or less logically from what had gone before.

Cohabitation

To begin with, if premarital sex is okay, then what objection could there be to unmarried sexual cohabitation? Could we say that it is okay for an unmarried couple to have sex, and to have sex frequently, but these sexual encounters must not take place in an apartment they share? Of course not. If frequent premarital sex is morally okay, then how can its location matter—provided, needless to say, that it takes place in a private place concealed from the eyes of the public? Once fornication won widespread acceptance among the young, it was not long before cohabitation (or "shacking up") also won widespread acceptance.

So great has the acceptance of cohabitation become in recent decades that it is now an almost mandatory preliminary to marriage. Millions will think you are a bit "strange" if you do not live with your future spouse for a year or two prior to your wedding. Isn't it only prudent to have what amounts to "trial marriage" before committing yourself to the real thing? Isn't that a way to reduce the likelihood of eventual divorce?

Promiscuity

At the beginning of the sexual revolution, love or affection was generally thought to be a condition needed to give moral legitimacy to premarital sex. But this phase of the fornication stage of the sexual revolution didn't last long. If all the other arguments in favor of premarital sex were sound, would not the overall argument remain sound even if we dropped the "love" portion of the argument? If two college students who are 100% in love one another can have sex, why can't two college students go to bed with one another even though they are only 90% in love? And if 90%, why not 80%? Why not 70% or 60% or all the way down to 1%?

That logic led to the widespread belief that there can be no moral objection to casual sex or sex with many partners. In short there can be no objection to sexual promiscuity—provided of course that realistic precautions are taken against pregnancy and disease.

This is not to say that many young people actually engaged in promiscuous sex. You might get rid of the "old-fashioned" notion that premarital sex is morally wrong, but promiscuity may well not be to your taste. Or even if you are willing to engage in promiscuity, the opportunities to do so may not arise. Or perhaps such opportunities may arise for exceptional young persons, e.g., a young man who is a star athlete on campus, but not many others. And only a very rare young woman, whether because of social conditioning or because modesty is built into the feminine half of human nature, would think of promiscuity as being in any way ideal.

Despite this, despite the fact that not a great number of young people became *actually* promiscuous, once they accepted the principle that premarital sex is morally okay, indeed is morally good, they had no good theoretical reason to object to loveless sex or to sex with many partners. As a result, among unmarried young people during the last half-century, although there has not been a great deal of downright promiscuous sex, there has been significant amount of not-very-loving sex with more than a few partners.

One of the long-term results of this tolerance of promiscuity has been the current campaign (I'm writing this in the year 2022) among many sexual revolutionists to legalize prostitution. If promiscuous sex is morally okay, what objection can there be to getting paid for having promiscuous sex?

Unmarried Parenthood

In the days prior to the sexual revolution (in the 1950s, let's say) an unmarried girl who "got in trouble"—that is, who became pregnant (yes, there were such happenings despite the rather puritanical morality of the era)—would feel ashamed of herself, or at all events she was expected to feel ashamed of herself. The great problem with an unmarried pregnancy was that it revealed to the public, or at least to the girl's family, friends, schoolmates, teachers, and neighbors, that she had done a very naughty thing on at least one occasion, and probably more than one: she had had sexual intercourse while unmarried; she had lost her virginity with a boy (or man) with whom she was not married. This was a serious sin, and among the middle classes and those lower-class people with middle class aspirations, a very serious sin.

There were four options available to a young woman who found herself "in trouble" (as the popular expression was).

(1) She could give birth to the baby and raise it as her own. But in those days this was *nearly* unthinkable. So it rarely happened.

(2) She could have an abortion. But this was nearly unthinkable. Everywhere in the USA it was a criminal offense to perform an abortion. And it was generally considered very wicked either to perform an abortion or to undergo one. It was widely considered to be a kind of homicide. And so the vast majority of girls "in trouble" did not resort to abortion—though some did, and some self-provoked a miscarriage, and many attempted to provoke a miscarriage.

(3) She could insist that the father of the baby marry her prior to the birth of the baby. The father might be reluctant to marry the girl, for the father was usually nothing more than a boy. But it was generally understood that this was "the right thing" for a man/boy to do, and so his conscience, along with some prodding from the girl, her parents, and his own parents, would often lead him to do this. And if his conscience was not strong enough, heavy pressure would be brought to bear, resulting in a so-called "shotgun wedding."

(4) She could give birth and put the baby up for adoption, turning the baby over to an adoption agency very soon after birth. This

was a respectable option; it was socially approved of; although painful for the young mother, it was a great relief for the young father and for the parents of both the mother and the father; and it was often the most sensible option available. The mother by so doing would avoid wedding an immature boy. Although she would give up her parental rights and would never know who adopted the baby, she could hope, probably realistically, that the baby had been adopted by a good married couple. And she could get on with her life.

But once premarital sex came to seem morally right in the eyes of society, there need be no shame in being pregnant without having a husband. An unmarried pregnancy might be unfortunate or inconvenient in a number of ways, but it was no longer shameful, for the sexual act that had brought it about was no longer shameful. Or if it was shameful, it was so only in the eyes of older people, out-of-date people who did not yet recognize the moral validity of the sexual revolution. But in the eyes of up-to-date younger persons, the peers of the pregnant girl, there was little shame in being pregnant and unmarried. Of course her friends might think a pregnant unmarried young woman was really dumb for allowing herself to become pregnant or to become pregnant by this or that particular man—but they did not hold it against her that she had engaged in an act of premarital sex.

This new situation created by the social acceptability of premarital sex greatly lessened the pregnant woman's motive for putting the baby up for adoption; it also lessened her motive for persuading the father of the baby to marry her.

The end result of all this is that tremendous numbers of young women who became pregnant without a husband decided to give birth without being married and to raise the child on their own. In other words, millions of girls, many of them poor and badly educated, and many of them "persons of color," decided to be unwed mothers.

This has been a social disaster in many ways. Unmarried motherhood usually means that boys and girls are growing up without their fathers being in the home, and without the support that fathers are supposed to provide: emotional and financial support, moral and religious and educational guidance, etc. Of course the single mother can provide some of this support and guidance; but two parents living together in the home will normally be able to do this better than a single parent. Further, a growing boy needs an intimate day-by-day connection with his father if the boy is to learn what it is to be a "real" man. Absent a father, the boy will seek his models of manhood elsewhere. And where will he find them? Often among the older boys of his neighborhood, and if it is a poor neighborhood (as it often will be since his single mother will not have the resources to live in a better neighborhood), the older boys will also have grown up fatherless, and as a result they will have a distorted idea—a stupid caricature—of what a "real man" is like. They will imagine that real masculinity involves being "tough" and having loveless sex with many women. The boy may well become part of a delinquent gang. As he grows older he will get in trouble with the police and will get a few girls pregnant. The cycle of unsuccess will begin again.

Girls too need a father. They too need to know what a "real man" is. Lacking that knowledge, a knowledge that can be best gained by daily contact with a father who is himself a real man, a girl is in danger of getting involved with morally and psychologically defective men who pretend to be real men. She is in danger of getting pregnant by a man who, instead of marrying her, goes to prison.

Abortion

As unmarried sexual intercourse became increasingly acceptable in the eyes of public opinion in the 1960s and '70s, so did abortion. After all, as unmarried sex became more and more common in those decades, so did unintended pregnancies. You may take "precautions," but the use of contraceptives, even by intelligent people who know what they are doing, is not one hundred percent effective. And it is not effective at all when it is not used, which is often the case when the sex partners are young and uneducated—when for example they are high school kids. In a moral regime of sexual freedom unintended pregnancies are bound to happen from time to time. What then?

Moral conservatives, who are usually orthodox Catholics or Evangelical Protestants, say that we should retreat from the sexual revolution and make a return to old-fashioned chastity. Champions of the sexual revolution say that is impossible, and they assert that it would not be desirable even if it were possible. We need better sex education, they say, we need free condoms and other contraceptives, and we need abortion as a backup when all else fails. We cannot have a moral regime of sexual freedom unless we have legal abortion as a backup. Abortion is an indispensable factor in the sexual revolution.

Public opinion, by which in this context I mean *liberal* public opinion, had arrived at this conclusion by the late 1960s and early '70s. And this liberal opinion was ratified by the US Supreme Court in January of 1973 when it announced its *Roe v. Wade* decision, declaring that the US Constitution contains an implied right to abortion. With that ruling, almost every state law in the nation banning or restricting abortion was struck down as un-Constitutional. The triumph of sexual freedom was now coupled with the triumph of virtually unlimited abortion.

Further, the Supreme Court ruling in *Roe* did not simply signify that abortion was legally permitted. It implied that it was morally permitted too. For the traditional Western idea of natural or human rights, an idea going back in America at least to the US Declaration of Independence if not further, is that these rights are God-given things ("endowed by their Creator"). And so the typical American had come to believe that the rights guaranteed by the US Constitution are God-given rights; from which it follows that if, as the Court said in *Roe*, abortion is a Constitutional right, then it must be a God-given right; and if it is a God-given right, then having an abortion must be morally correct.

Homosexuality

If we as a society are to grant heterosexuals the right to have sex with whomever they want and whenever they want, would not it be unfair to deny a similar freedom to gays and lesbians and bisexuals? Of course. And so homosexual freedom followed logically from heterosexual freedom. But there was a lag time between public acceptance of heterosexual freedom and public acceptance of homosexual freedom. After all, gays and lesbians were only a small percentage of the population (about 2% or 3% at most); their wishes could safely be ignored, at least for a while. But not forever.

The June 1969 Stonewall Riots in Greenwich Village marked the beginning of a strong gay rights movement. In every big city in America, above all in New York City and San Francisco, there was a significant enclave (or "ghetto") of homosexual men plus a smaller number of homosexual women. Using these population centers as its base, and using as its principal resource the considerable intellectual and creative talents often found among homosexuals, and using the support given to it by (heterosexual) moral and political liberals, the gay rights movement gradually became a great force in American social and political life. The movement's first demand was that homosexual relationships be tolerated by the non-homosexual world—tolerated by law, by custom, and by the police. Correlative with this demand was a demand made *within* the homosexual world, the demand that gays and lesbians "come out of the closet." And so they did. In tremendous numbers. In many cases this was a painful coming-out, especially when the homosexual person shocked and disappointed his/her parents.

By and large, however, American society was not shocked. For the most part people were tolerant, and they grew more tolerant as the years went by. The black civil rights movement of the 1950s and '60s had taught Americans a great lesson in tolerance and in the evils of intolerance and bigotry. And so when the gay rights movement came along, it made the strategically wise decision to present itself as a movement asking that people be tolerant of yet another minority group which, like blacks, had been historically victimized by prejudice and discrimination. Homosexual activists did not say, "We want you to be tolerant of certain kinds of sexual conduct that you have hitherto been intolerant of." No, they said instead, "We want you to be tolerant of a certain minority group—a group of people who, like blacks, are what they are through no choice of their own (they are "born that way")—that you have hitherto, because of bigotry and hatred, been intolerant of."

The AIDS crisis of the 1980s looked at first as though it might do great damage to the gay rights movement. This terrible disease was concentrated among gay men, especially young gay men, many of whom were reveling in their new freedom by being sexually promiscuous, having scores, in some cases even hundreds, of sex partners. While the gay movement was arguing that homosexuality was "virtually normal,"[2] anti-gays could have argued that homosexuality, or at least male homosexuality, is far from normal if it gives society the dreadful AIDS epidemic. They *could* have made this argument. But not many did—and those who did, did not find many listeners. Just the opposite. In a brilliant strategic move, the gay rights movement utilized the AIDS epidemic to win great sympathy for gays, telling sad stories of gay men who had fallen victim to the awful plague, and telling edifying stories of other gay men who had lovingly nursed these victims as they died slowly and painfully. It was as if the victims were heroic soldiers who had died at the hands of a cruel and aggressive enemy. Little mention was made of the fact that in almost all cases the "victims" were victims of their own reckless sexual conduct—conduct which at an earlier and less "tolerant" time would have been called immoral and unnatural.

The gay rights movement in the USA was strongly critical of the Reagan administration for failing to produce a cure or a preventive vaccine; a criticism that was welcomed by non-gay liberals who despised the Regan administration. And the movement derided the Catholic Church and Protestant Evangelical churches for continuing to teach "homophobia" (gay-hatred) to their people even while tens of thousands of innocent gay men, piteous sights, were lying on their deathbeds. The representatives of old-fashioned Christianity were blamed and ridiculed for their lack of the fundamental Christian virtue, love of neighbor.

Supporters of the gay movement, many of them atheists or near-atheists, proclaimed that they understood the morality of Jesus better than did the self-described followers of Jesus. True

[2] The title of a book by Andrew Sullivan, a prominent writer on social and political topics who is quite openly gay. (Sullivan, *Virtually Normal*, Vintage Books, 1995.)

Christian love was found, not in the churches, but in the AIDS-stricken gay community.

And when Christians said, as they often did, "We hate the sin, but we love the sinner," the gay rights movement often responded: "No, you hate gays and lesbians, and that is why you hate their so-called 'sins.' When these 'sins' are committed by heterosexuals, you don't care."

As years passed, the gay movement won significant legislative battles in state after state; one state after another enacting laws banning discrimination in employment, education, and housing on the basis of sexual orientation. A great legal victory for the gay rights movement came on 26 March 2003, when the US Supreme Court ruled in a 6-3 decision (*Lawrence v. Texas*) that all laws banning homosexual intercourse are invalid since the US Constitution implicitly protects the right to engage in such conduct.[3] The implication was that homosexual sodomy is a God-given right.

Next the gay rights movement demanded that same-sex marriage ("marriage equality" as its supporters call it) be recognized by law. Beginning in the first decade of the twenty-first century a number of states did so recognize it, and finally, in June 2015, the US Supreme Court, in a 5-4 ruling (*Obergefell v. Hodges*) declared that the Constitution of the USA contains an implicit right to same-sex marriage. One more God-given right. Of course the Constitution does not explicitly contain such a right; it says nothing about marriage and nothing about homosexuality; further, marriage had traditionally been something that the states, and the states alone, could regulate. But according to the Court the Constitution (at least if you torture it enough)[4] contains an implicit right to same-sex marriage.

Homo-conformity

You would think that a Constitutional right to marry a same-sex partner would be the end of the demands made by the gay rights

---

[3] The Court said this despite the fact that the US Constitution says not a single word about sex or homosexuality.

[4] This of course is *my* opinion, not the Court's.

movement. I mean, what more could it ask for? But if you thought that, you would be wrong. Nowadays the gay movement holds, and its liberal/progressive allies agree, that anti-gay sentiment (homophobia or gay-hatred) is as bad a thing as racism, and it has no more right to exist than does racism. Homophobia must be eradicated, not just from the behavior and overt conduct of Americans, but also from American hearts and minds. You and I are not entitled to have anti-homosexuality thoughts or feelings. And if we happen to have them, we had better keep them strictly concealed; we must not reveal them by slips of the tongue or by making or laughing at improper jokes. And if we happen to have such homophobic thoughts or feelings, and we are so careless as not to keep them totally concealed, we should be punished—perhaps with a reprimand, perhaps by getting fired, perhaps by having our career and reputation totally destroyed. Schools should support pro-gay sentiments. Schoolkids should be taught (that is, propagandized) to believe that homosexual conduct is a perfectly fine thing and that anybody who disagrees is a hater.

What began decades ago as a crusade for tolerance has evolved into an intolerant demand for what may be called homo-conformity.

Incidentally, this demand for homo-conformity is tantamount to a demand for the rejection of old-fashioned Christianity, the kind of Christianity found in the Catholic Church and in most Protestant Evangelical denominations. For old-fashioned Christianity condemns homosexual practice, just as it condemns many other sexual practices sanctioned by the sexual revolution. And the sexual code of old-fashioned Christianity is not a merely incidental or ornamental feature of the religion. On the contrary, a high standard of chastity has always lain very near the heart of Christianity. Reject this standard, and you reject Christianity itself. When public schools teach, as many of them do, that homosexual conduct is right and proper and that same-sex marriage is equally right and proper, they are teaching, by very clear implication, that Christianity—at least as Christianity as understood by Catholics and Evangelical Protestants—is a false and wicked religion.

Transgenderism

At some point along the way the gay rights movement renamed itself the LGBT movement, these letters standing for Lesbian-Gay-Bisexual-Transgender. And then it renamed itself again, changing LGBT to LGBTQ, the letter Q standing for Queer. Often the five letters are followed by a "plus" sign: LGBTQ+, the "plus" sign indicating an indefinite multitude of further sexual practices or identities. Some people think there should be two Qs (LGBTQQ), one for "queer" and the other for "questioning."

According to the sexual left, gender identity is something quite different from biological/anatomical sex. You may have been born with a penis, but that does not mean that you are a boy; or you may have been born with a vagina, but that does not mean that you are a girl. When we say that the baby with a penis is a boy, we are "assigning" a gender to the newborn; and when we say that the baby without a penis is a girl, we are "assigning" a gender to the newborn.

But an assigned gender is not a person's "true" gender; a person's "true" gender is the one that he/she/it personally adopts. How can it be otherwise? In a genuinely free society (which the USA claims to be), how can it be that others—parents, medical personnel, friends, neighbors, schoolteachers, cops, storekeepers, etc.—have the right to tell me what my gender is? No, that is a right that should be reserved to myself. If I say that I am a boy or a man, then I am a boy or a man, regardless of what gender other persons may wish to assign to me. Likewise if I say that I am a girl or a woman. Further, if I announce that I am neither male nor female but that I am of some third, fourth, or even fifth or some other of a potentially infinite number of genders, then I am of the gender I assign to myself. If personal freedom means anything at all, it means the freedom to choose one's gender.

Now most people, it so happens, choose for themselves the gender identity that others (e.g., parents) have assigned to them. That is okay—provided their choice is a free choice. One wonders, however, how much freedom has been involved in making that choice. If I happen to be born with a penis, and if as a result of this accident of birth everybody treats me as boy throughout the many years of my growing-up, how free have I really been to make the fateful decision as to my true gender? In a better world, the world (let us hope) of our future, children will be reminded early in life (maybe at the age of 2 or 3 or 4) that they themselves, not somebody else, will make the final decision as to whether they will be boys or girls or some third thing.

In practice nowadays, persons who choose a gender identity other than the gender identity assigned to them at birth usually do so because they "feel" themselves to be of a gender that differs from their assigned gender. Some people feel themselves to be boys "trapped" in a girl's body, or girls "trapped" in a boy's body—or adult men "trapped" in the body of an adult woman, or adult women "trapped" in the body of an adult male—or a person of some non-male and non-female third gender "trapped" in a male or female body. This feeling has been called "gender dysphoria," and it used to be considered a kind of mental/emotional illness—just as homosexuality used to be considered a kind of mental/emotional illness.

Decades ago, liberal or progressive thinkers in the world of psychology and psychiatry decided that such thoughts about homosexuality were badly mistaken; that there is nothing "ill" or "diseased" about same-sex attractions or homosexual intercourse; that homosexuality is just as "natural" as heterosexuality. The time has come, argue the advocates of transgenderism, to acknowledge that there is nothing "ill" or "diseased" about gender dysphoria. It is perfectly fine, both health-wise and morality-wise, for a person to become aware that he or she was born into the wrong body, and it is perfectly reasonable for a person to demand that society treat him or her according to the gender of his or her choice. And it is quite unfair, quite un-American, and quite un-Christian for others to refuse to comply with this demand.

What is more, just as public schools now teach children that homosexuality is morally and psychologically unobjectionable, so they must teach the same about transgenderism. They must teach schoolchildren that only bigotry, hate, or stupidity, or a combination of all three motivates some persons (conservatives) to oppose transgenderism.

If a trans man (that is, a biological woman who believes herself to be a man) is a man, then it follows that a man can have a vagina, can menstruate, can become pregnant, and can give birth. And if a trans woman (that is, a biological man who believes himself to be a man) is a woman, it follows that a woman can have a penis and testes, can have an erection, can produce semen, and can get a woman pregnant.

The earlier steps in the sexual revolution (fornication, cohabitation, homosexuality, abortion, etc.) had to do with sexual behavior. This new step—transgenderism—has to do, not with sexual behavior, but with sexual identity. Yet it is not without its connection to sexual behavior. For if a trans man is a man and a trans woman is a woman, then questions arise as to propriety of sexual intercourse between transgendered persons and biologically gendered persons.

A new word has been coined to deal with this issue. If you are inclined to have sexual relations with both biological men and biological women, you are (as we have been told for decades now) "bisexual." But if, going beyond mere bisexuality, you are inclined to have sexual relations with biological men and biological woman and transmen and transwomen, you are, we now learn, "pansexual."

Moral conservatives (including the author of this book) object to transgenderism for a number of reasons, foremost among them being the following.

1. We believe that persons who believe themselves to be members of the sex opposite their biological sex are suffering from a mental illness or at least from a serious personality disorder.

2. We believe that non-transgender persons who give their support to the transgender movement are leftist ideologues who, in order to advance their ideology, are willing to promote ideas that they know deep down to be false—reminiscent of those leftists who used to pretend to believe that Communist Russia was a humane and democratic society.

3. We believe that the transgender ideology will do significant damage to sports for girls and women. Males who are stronger or taller or faster or heavier will, after declaring themselves to be

female, win all the big prizes. Women will have to go back to pie-making contests.

4. We believe that the ideology will permit (indeed is already permitting) trans girls and trans women (that is, biological boys and men) to use locker rooms and showers and public restrooms that have hitherto been reserved for real girls and real women. In other words, real girls and women will be subject to great embarrassment (and who knows what else?) in order to accommodate the delusions of certain mentally ill males and the ideology of leftist adults.

5. More importantly, we believe that under the influence of this widespread transgender ideology, adolescence—which even in the best of times is a period of psychological turbulence for kids—will now be a period of even greater turbulence. How many of you adults reading this book would wish to return to the psychological stresses and strains, many of them related to a developing sexuality, that you experienced when you were 12 or 13 or 14 or 15 years old? Well, kids who are pre-teens today will in a few years have to worry, not just about the perennial things that you and I worried about, but about gender identity too. They will lie awake at night wondering, "Am I a boy or a girl?" In the old days you could answer this question by glancing at what you had between your legs. Now kids will feel enormous pressure to ask themselves, "What is my true gender identity, hidden deep within my soul?"

How cruel of leftists to inflict this notable increment of mental pain on growing kids. Cruelest of all are those parents—those monsters of iniquity I should rather say—who for the sake of being fashionably avant-garde encourage their six- and seven- and eight-year-olds to claim a gender identity that is in conflict with their biological sex. "Look at me," these parents say, "I have a trans kid. I'm super-cool. Don't you envy me?"

6. Finally, we object to the "philosophy" that underlies all this, a philosophy that says that nothing is what it is; rather, it is what we *say* it is. Everything is a "construct"—constructed either by society or by some social group or by the autonomous individual. And so believers in this philosophy can *say* (as do pro-abortionists) that a fetus is not a human being; and kill it. And so believers

in this philosophy can also *say* (as did Nazis) that Jews are subhuman; and kill them.

"After all," believers in this inhuman philosophy can say, "what is freedom if we are not free to construct our thought-world as we please? And what good is freedom if the weirdest members of society are not free to inflict their delusions on others?"

13

Religious Decline

A multitude of social, cultural, economic, and political factors have contributed to the many successes of the modern sexual revolution. In this and the next two chapters I will discuss three of them: in this chapter Religious Decline; in the next two chapters Moral Liberalism and Liberal Protestantism.

In the immediate post-World War II years there was a notable religious revival in the USA, especially a Christian revival, both Protestant and Catholic.

1. In the world of Evangelical Protestantism Billy Graham (1918–2018) was the outstanding figure. His revivals were drawing immense crowds, not just in the "backwoods" areas where Protestant fundamentalism had long flourished (Graham came out of this fundamentalist tradition), but in big cities like New York and Los Angeles and even London.

2. In mainline Protestantism the big name was Reinhold Niebuhr (1892–1971), who had, one might almost say, "rediscovered" Original Sin, something that had been more or less forgotten among the liberal Christians who had dominated American Protestantism since the 1920s. Niebuhr, with his vivid awareness of the sinfulness of human nature, had been able to account for the evils of Communism and Nazis, and many lesser evils, in a way that liberal Protestants, with their idea that human nature is fundamentally good, could never do. Niebuhr had replaced Harry Emerson Fosdick, a champion of liberal or modernist Protestantism, as the foremost Protestant thinker of the day.

3. In Catholicism the most conspicuous public figure of the era was Bishop Fulton J. Sheen (1895–1979), whose great learning

and great eloquence were on display for the entire nation, not just Catholics, on his weekly TV program "Life is Worth Living." The 1950s was, we may say, the "golden age" of American Catholicism. American Catholics, a minority long viewed with skepticism and disapproval by the American Protestant majority, had finally come into their own. Their sacrifices during World War II, equal to Protestant sacrifices, had removed all doubt as to their Americanism. They were flourishing socially, politically and economically. The election in 1960 of one of their own, John F. Kennedy, to the presidency was a striking sign that at long last they had truly *arrived* in the USA. Their churches were overflowing with parishioners, and they were building new parish churches all the time. The same with Catholic schools, both elementary and high school. Catholic colleges were numerous and flourishing, and growing more numerous every year. The Church abounded in priests, religious sisters, and religious brothers.[1]

What were the social causes of this religious revival of the late '40s and 1950s? No doubt there were many causes, as there are many causes for any historical change; but let me point out two of them. (a) The United States had just come through two of the most trying times in its history, the Great Depression of the 1930s and World War II in the first half of the '40s. The religious revival, it seems to me, was in part an act of gratitude, a way of thanking God that he had saved the country. (b) In the aftermath of the war, a new "war" had emerged, the Cold War between the USA (and its allies) and the Soviet Union (and its satellite nations). There were numerous differences between the USA and Communist Russia. For instance, a democratic political system versus a totalitarian system. Again, a capitalistic or free enterprise economic system versus a socialistic/authoritarian economic system. Further, Russia was officially an atheistic society and culture (even though, as we learned after the fall of Communism in 1991, many Russians had retained their old religious beliefs during the long atheistic decades), while the United States, by contrast, was (unofficially) a

[1] Sadly, this golden age would come to an end in the 1960s and '70s. See my book *The Decline and Fall of the Catholic Church in America* (Sophia Institute Press, 2003).

God-fearing and mostly Christian country. During the Cold War, especially during the early years of the Cold War, it was a patriotic thing to be religious; it was a way of saying, "I love America and I detest atheistic Communism."

But then came the 1960s and the emergence of a new generation, the so-called "baby boom" generation, whose members had known neither the Great Depression nor World War II. What is more, the Soviet Union was no longer as scary as it had been while Stalin was alive (he had died in March 1953); and following the Cuban Missile Crisis of November 1962 relations between the USA and the USSR settled down into a relatively stable antagonism. The decade was marked by the Black Civil Rights movement, by the Viet Nam War and strong opposition to it, and by a generalized opposition by young people to all forms of authority—political, police, academic, parental, and religious.

The postwar religious revival came to an end in the 1960s. American Catholicism went into decline. Mainline Protestantism went into an even greater decline. Evangelical (or conservative or fundamentalist) Protestantism remained strong. And so did Mormonism.

As a result, many in the younger generation became receptive to an atheistic or near-atheistic worldview, and to a sexual morality that was consistent with that worldview.

14

Moral Liberalism

Underlying the sexual revolution, and justifying it in the eyes of its supporters and sympathizers, is a theory of morality—a philosophical theory—that became enormously popular in the USA soon after the sexual revolution began, especially among young persons, but not only among young persons. This theory may be called *moral liberalism*. It is composed of two principles:

- The Personal Liberty Principle (PLP), according to which a person is morally free to do whatever he or she wishes—provided no harm is done to another person.
- The Tolerance Principle, according to which we are morally bound to tolerate the conduct of other persons provided they act in accordance with the personal liberty principle; in other words, provided they do no harm to others.

However, to understand the fine points of moral liberalism we must bear a few things in mind.

- Moral liberalism applies to adults, not to children. However, moral liberals have no agreement as to where the line is to be drawn between childhood and adulthood.
- The harm in question must be one (or more) of four kinds:
    - Economic harm (e.g., I rob a bank, I pick your pocket, I commit arson).
    - Bodily harm (e.g., I break your leg, I commit rape or murder).
    - Reputational harm (e.g., I commit libel or slander).
    - Emotional harm (I do serious damage to your feelings).
- The harm in question must be harm to somebody other than oneself. If you wish to harm yourself, or if you wish to en-

gage in conduct that creates a notable risk of harm to yourself (e.g., using drugs, engaging in sexual promiscuity), well, that is up to you. After all, it is your life, your body. If you are an adult you can do with your life and your body as you like.

- The harm in question must be such as to be either obvious (e.g., I push you down the stairs or pick your pocket) or provable scientifically (e.g., smoking has a high probability of leading to lung cancer or some other serious disease).
- Merely spiritual or religious harm does not count as harm (this means I have not harmed you if I induce you to skip church on Sunday, or if I persuade you to cease believing in God, or if I seduce you into a voluntary act of fornication or adultery).
- Harm that is consented to by the "victim" does not count as harm. For instance, you allow a surgeon to cut you open; or you are a masochist who consents to be the recipient of sadistic abuse.

Moral liberalism justified, or at least *seemed* to justify in the eyes of tens of millions of persons, especially young persons, forms of conduct characteristic of the sexual revolution—I mean, fornication, abortion, homosexuality, etc. And thus we found, and still find today, sexual liberationists (if we may give that name to the proponents of the sexual revolution) again and again appealing to moral liberalism arguments to justify the non-traditional sexual conduct they approved of. They say things like these:

- "What harm does it do if a college boy and college girl go to bed with one another, provided they take precautions against unwanted pregnancy?"
- "How does it harm *you* if two gay men or two lesbians go to bed with one another? Or if they marry one another? Will this hurt *your* marriage? Will your wife announce that she is divorcing you or that she will no longer cook your dinner because two men across the street are having gay sex with one another?"
- "How does it harm anybody if a young woman, wishing to continue uninterrupted with her career or her education, terminates her pregnancy?"

This last one—abortion—presents something of a problem for sexual liberationists. It is obvious that abortion does great harm to another person, indeed lethal harm; for it kills an unborn human being. How do sexual liberationists get around this difficulty? Typical of their answers are some of the following.

- They simply deny that the unborn baby is a human being.
- When an abortion takes place early in the pregnancy, the aborted embryo is no bigger than a peanut; and a thing as small as a peanut cannot possibly be a human person.
- The judgment as to whether or not a fetus is a human being is a subjective judgment; it is not the recognition of an objective fact. If you judge that the thing being aborted is human, you should abstain from abortion; if you think it is not human, you are morally free to go ahead with an abortion.
- The unborn baby *may* be a human being, but nobody can be sure of this; and in the absence of certainty we are entitled to kill the thing.
- We may kill the unborn baby in self-defense, for it is an unjust aggressor, like an enemy who intends to do us harm.
- The right of a woman to control her own body—this is usually spoken of as a right to "bodily autonomy"—is a supreme value, trumping any right the unborn baby may happen to have. ("My body, my choice.")

If these are not good arguments (and they are not), this does not discourage sexual liberationists from using them today, just as it has not discouraged them for fifty or sixty years now. If good arguments are not available, they will simply have to use bad arguments. For from the sexual liberationist point of view, abortion is an indispensable element of the sexual revolution, and if it cannot be defended with good arguments it will have to be defended with bad. And if it cannot be defended with either good or bad arguments, it will have to be defended with bumper-sticker slogans: for instance, "Keep your rosaries off my ovaries" or "My body, my choice" or "If you don't like abortions, don't have one." Absent abortion, the whole sexual revolution will be in danger of collapsing. If there is no legal abortion available to take care of "mistakes," many women and even many men will be more cautious about having sexual intercourse with anybody but their spouses.

And who knows where this increased caution may lead? It may even lead in the direction of a reversal of the sexual revolution. Worse still, it may lead to a rediscovery of the Christian virtue of chastity. Hence, the legal and moral right to abortion must be defended no matter what.

In passing we may note that when pro-life (or anti-abortion) people describe prochoice people as being "pro-abortion," the latter often indignantly respond by saying one of two things. (a) First, "I am not pro-abortion"—meaning, "I personally would never have an abortion, but I want that option to be available to other women who may feel differently." (b) Or second, "Nobody is *pro*-abortion"—meaning, "Nobody *likes* abortion; nobody undergoes abortion for its own sake. Women have abortions out of sad necessity, not for the fun of it."

Now these would be good responses if the pro-life people were saying what the pro-choice people imagine them to be saying. But they are not. When Mrs. Pro-life says to Ms. Pro-choice, "You are not simply in favor of choice, you are in favor of abortion," Ms. Pro-life is not asserting that Ms. Pro-choice is herself willing to undergo an abortion; nor is she asserting that prochoice people think it's a pleasant thing to have an abortion. Not at all.

What Ms. Pro-life is asserting is that Ms. Pro-choice is a supporter of the *institution* of abortion; a supporter, in other words, of the US Supreme Court ruling (*Roe v. Wade*) that made abortion legal in 1973, and of the readiness of law enforcement authorities to protect the legal right to abortion, and of the clinics and hospitals and doctors who perform abortions and nurses and others who assist them in this homicidal work.

An analogy may be made with slavery. If we were living in the USA in the 1850s, and we said that Mr. X is pro-slavery, we would be speaking the truth even if he personally owned no slaves and refused to own a slave—provided he was in favor of the *institution* of slavery. Suppose he said, "I hate slavery; I'd rather die than own a slave." But let us suppose he also said, "I believe in the right to own slaves, and I believe that the power of the government should be used to protect that right, and I believe that the Congress and the President should do nothing to interfere with that right"—such a man could fairly be described as pro-slavery.

When I say that the principle of moral liberalism leads to a justification of the sexual revolution, I do not mean to describe a chronological relationship, but rather a logical relationship. Logically, moral liberalism comes first; fornication, out-of-wedlock births, homosexuality, abortion, and all the other content of the sexual revolution follow as deductions from moral liberalism: if it is right, they are right. But chronologically that is not how it happened. The sexual revolution began with college boys and girls going to bed with one another. But a justification was needed for this rather novel practice. Moral liberalism was seized on as a justification (or at least an apparent justification) of undergraduate fornication. But once the theory of moral liberalism was embraced, it was soon noted that it would justify much more than mere fornication. And so this theory led to a great expansion of the sexual revolution—an expansion that led to approval of all the other elements of the ongoing sexual revolution.

The reader will no doubt have noted that many of the *apparently* harmless practices that have been endorsed by the sexual revolution's use of moral liberalism are not in fact harmless, even though they are counted as harmless in order to pass the moral liberalism test.

Sexual liberationists say that fornication, homosexuality, abortion, etc. do no harm. They bring joy to the world or at least (in the case of abortion) relief from pain. Hmmm. But what about the tremendous number of sexually transmitted diseases that we have in America—and not just HIV/AIDS, the greatest "celebrity" among these multitudinous diseases? And what about the tremendous number of kids growing up without fathers, many of these kids later ending up in poverty and in prison? And what about the more than sixty million abortions that have taken place since *Roe v. Wade* in 1973? Can the liberationists honestly say that the sexual revolution has been a harmless thing?

Well, it so happens that the liberationists have answers for all these objections. These are very poor answers, and they are answers that will not satisfy an unprejudiced judge, but they seem to satisfy the liberationists themselves; the answers serve to quiet the conscience of enthusiasts for the sexual revolution. Their answers to the difficulties raised in the preceding paragraph fall into three categories:

1. They argue that some of these apparent harms are not real harms. Take, for instance, those sixty million abortions; they are not sixty million bad things, they are sixty million good things; not good in themselves ("nobody is *pro* abortion"), but good in their consequences; good as means, not as ends.
2. They argue that many of the ill effects of abortion are a price we have to pay for the great benefits we obtain from sexual freedom, a price we should be willing pay since the benefits vastly outweigh the cost; just as the benefits of automobiles are paid for in tens of thousands of annual deaths from auto accidents.
3. They argue that the spread of sexually transmitted diseases can be slowed down and even eliminated if governments at every level, federal, state, and local, will take a few simple steps. And what are these steps?

- Provide kids with sex education programs, beginning probably in kindergarten, that will teach these kids to be tolerant of all kinds of consensual sexual behavior, from which it will follow that nobody need feel shame for any sex act he or she engages in.
- By means of rational sex education programs, assure that kids when they grow up (that is, when they are 14 or 15 or 16) will never have unprotected sex.
- Provide kids and adults, especially girls and women, with free-of-charge contraception. And provide them with free-of-charge abortion when "mistakes" are made.
- As for the millions of fatherless children that result from sexual freedom, provide single mothers and their kids with adequate social welfare programs, e.g., food stamps, Medicaid, rental subsidies, free daycare for children, free pre-K education, free cell phones, free rides on buses and taxis, etc. And spend the money needed to make sure that public schools in low-income neighborhoods (where most of these single mothers live) are as

good as public schools in well-to-do suburbs.

- The federal government should launch a tremendous "war on STDs," finding medicines that will quickly heal these diseases when they occur and, more important, developing vaccines to prevent the rise of these diseases in the first place.

If all these things were to be done, liberationists argue, the sexual revolution would produce almost no harmful side effects. Done the right way, sexual freedom will be an overwhelmingly positive thing and will make a tremendous contribution to the happiness and well-being of the American people. The problem is not sexual freedom; the problem is carelessness and stupidity. Anything—sex or anything else—will have harmful effects if done carelessly and stupidly. Get rid of carelessness and stupidity, and sexual freedom will be a glorious thing.

15

Liberal Protestantism

If moral liberalism has made great contributions to the spread of the sexual revolution, so has liberal Protestantism.

The reader will remember, I hope, the distinction I made earlier in the book between liberal (or modernistic) Protestantism and conservative (or traditional) Protestantism. Liberal Protestantism is strongly present today in the so-called mainline Protestant denominations—e.g., The Episcopal Church, Evangelical Lutheran Church of America, Presbyterian Church USA, the American branch of the United Methodist Church, and the United Church of Christ.[1] Conservative Protestantism is to be found in Evangelical churches (the largest of which is the Southern Baptist Convention), in Pentecostal churches, and in the Lutheran Church/Missouri Synod. A morally conservative kind of Christianity is also found in the Church of Jesus Christ of Latter-Day Saints (the Mormons), a church that deviates widely from old-fashioned Protestantism in doctrine yet adheres closely to it in moral standards.

Liberal or modernistic Protestants, by contrast, taking advantage of—and greatly exaggerating or abusing—the old Protestant right of private judgment, feel free to reject any traditional Christian doctrine that does not make sense to them; and what "makes sense" to them is usually what makes sense to the fashionable secular opinion of the day. Hence many liberal Protestants have rejected such traditional articles of Christian doctrine as the Virgin

[1] The Unitarian-Universalist Association is still more liberal than any of these. But the UUA no longer considers itself to be a Christian church.

Birth, the Resurrection of Jesus, the Divinity of Christ, the Trinity, the Atonement, even Heaven and Hell. However, they usually have a vague, often very vague, belief in God (or in something they call God) and a great admiration for Jesus, that famous first-century Jewish prophet and moralist. The more radical among liberal Protestants also reject many traditional Christian teachings regarding sexual morality: they have little or no objection, for example, to fornication, unmarried cohabitation, abortion, homosexuality, and same-sex marriage. In sum, they have accommodated to the sexual revolution.

If we date the beginning of liberal Protestantism to the rise of Boston Unitarianism in the late eighteenth and early nineteenth centuries, this means that liberal Protestants have been present in the United States for something more than two hundred years. Throughout that time they have repeatedly exhibited the same pattern, which is as follows:

(1) They have paid careful attention to any great attack coming from the forces of anti-Christianity. There have been three such attacks: deism (eighteenth century); agnosticism (late nineteenth century); and the atheistic sexual revolution (late twentieth, early twenty-first centuries).

(2) They have concluded that there is much merit in each of these attacks, but not enough to lead them to abandon Christianity altogether.

(3) And so they have developed new and ever-evolving forms of Christianity, forms that attempt to blend Christianity with deism or agnosticism or the sexual revolution.

(4) As decades and centuries pass, the Christian contribution to this blend becomes less and less while the anti-Christianity contribution becomes greater and greater, until finally liberal Christianity bears more of a resemblance to atheism than it does to traditional Christianity. (Imagine mixing and drinking a series of gin-and-tonics. Each time the gin becomes greater, the tonic less, until finally it is nearly all gin with only a few drops of tonic. Today's liberal Protestant is drunk with anti-Christianity.)

(5) As liberal Protestants have come to believe less and less in traditional Christian doctrine, they have more and more come

to think that morality, not doctrine, is the essence of Christianity; morality is what Christianity is all about, doctrine is merely incidental.

(6) As time passes, the morality they believe in becomes less and less a Christian morality and more and more an atheistic morality; for instance, they accept sexual freedom, abortion, and homosexual sodomy—three things that have nothing to do with Christianity, everything to do with atheism.

I have said that liberal Protestants have always seen some merit in the fashionable anti-Christianity of the day, whether it was deism or agnosticism or atheism, but not so much merit as to abandon Christianity entirely. Instead they have tried to blend Christianity and anti-Christianity—to make, we may say, a synthesis between the two, albeit a remarkably incoherent synthesis. It is not surprising, then, that when the sexual revolution came along liberal Protestants said to themselves, "Hmm, this is shocking. But those sexual liberationists have a point. Our traditional sexual morality has been too strict, too absolute; it does not allow for reasonable exceptions. Let's loosen things up a bit."

One of the earliest expressions of this accommodationist attitude was a book by Joseph Fletcher (1905–91), *Situation Ethics: the New Morality* (Westminster Press, 1966). Fletcher was an Episcopal priest and a professor at the Episcopal Theology School, Cambridge MA. He argued in his book that there is only one absolute or exception-less commandment, "Love your neighbor as yourself." All the more specific commandments—do not steal, do not lie, do not murder, do not commit adultery, and so on—allow for exceptions when they conflict with the one and only absolute commandment. And when Jesus spoke of loving one's neighbor he was not speaking of *liking* your neighbor or of *feeling* the emotion of affection for your neighbor. No, he was speaking of doing what is for your neighbor's benefit; and indeed for the benefit of *all* your neighbors—Jews, Samaritans, Romans, Greeks, Americans, Canadians, Europeans, Third World persons, etc.

Fletcher was in fact a Christian Utilitarian. As Jeremy Bentham and his disciples said that we must act to promote the greatest *happiness* of the greatest number, so Fletcher said that we must, per the command of Jesus, act to promote the greatest *good* of the greatest number.

And so if the assassination of Hitler would benefit humankind generally, we may assassinate Hitler, indeed we *must* assassinate Hitler. Therefore it was right for Dietrich Bonhoeffer and others to make their July 1944 attempt to kill Hitler. By contrast, the assassination of Abraham Lincoln did not benefit mankind generally; just the opposite, it was harmful to mankind generally, and therefore it was wrong of John Wilkes Booth to murder President Lincoln. (These are not Fletcher's examples, but they could have been.)

Or take an example actually given by Fletcher (see pages 164-65 of his book). A German woman, married with a husband and children at home, was being held prisoner in a Russian prison camp immediately after World War II. The Russians were releasing pregnant women from the camp. This particular woman felt a strong duty to return home to her husband and children. And so she found a Russian guard who was kind enough to impregnate her. She was released. Pregnant, she went home to her family, eventually giving birth to the child. Her family, including her husband, welcomed her and her baby with joy. They accepted the baby as one of the family. Although normally adultery is wrong, being productive of more bad than good, in this instance, Fletcher argued, adultery was right, being productive of more good than bad.

Although Fletcher's argument could be used to support many deviations from traditional Christian morality, his book became something of a theological best-seller because it could be used to support deviations from traditional sexual morality. For at the moment his book was published (the mid-1960s) the topic of deviations from traditional sexual morality was very much "in the air." Nobody was talking about possible deviations from the traditional rules against, e.g., shoplifting, arson, mugging, bank robbery, or wife-beating. But everybody was talking about sex and asking, "Is it morally okay to do X or Y or Z?" Fletcher told Christians how, under certain circumstances, they could do X, Y, Z, and many other (apparently immoral) things while considering themselves to be good Christians.

By the way, in the years following publication of his *Situation Ethics* book, Fletcher became an atheist, and from 1974 to 1976 he was president of the Euthanasia Society of America.[2]

Another writer who made a considerable contribution to the advance of liberal Protestantism was John Shelby Spong (1931–2021), retired Episcopal bishop of Newark NJ. He admires Jesus, who was a very good and wise man—even though he was not God, was not born of a virgin, did not rise from the dead, and is not our Lord and Savior. Spong has written a series of books and given hundreds of lectures, both in the USA and elsewhere, devoted to the demolition of classical Christian doctrines. For the most part his books have sold well (Spong, it must be admitted, has a felicitous prose style) and his lectures have been well-attended since there is a great potential audience in the world looking for reasons to drop belief in Christian doctrine and morals while at the same time continuing to call oneself a Christian. If you are looking for Christian reasons for ceasing to believe in Christianity, Spong is your man. He has made it clear that he does not believe in a single article of the Nicene Creed, except possibly (just possibly) belief in something that may be called God. Spong says he believes in a "non-theistic" God—whatever that can mean; it sounds rather like saying that one believes in non-circular circles.

Yet he calls himself a Christian—a believer in a new and improved kind of Christianity.

Needless to say, Spong has endorsed the sexual revolution; that is to say, he has provided Christian justifications for fornication, unmarried cohabitation, adultery, abortion, and homosexuality—not to mention justifications for euthanasia. Let's look at his 1988 book: *Living in Sin: a Bishop Rethinks Human Sexuality* (HarperSanFrancisco).

Early in his book Spong lays down two premises that will inform everything that follows. First, Christianity is, or at least it should be, an *inclusive* religion. God is the God of *all* people, not just Jews, not just males, not just heterosexuals, not just people who systematically abstain from what Christianity has tradition-

[2] See the Wikipedia entry on Fletcher.

ally called sexual sin—but everybody. A new and improved Christianity will have to see itself as a religion for *all* people. Second, until just the other day (so to speak) women, who make up half the human race, have been regarded as inferior human beings, second-class persons, not entitled to the rights and freedoms that the other half, men, have traditionally been entitled to, including sexual rights and freedoms. We are now living in a new human era, the era of gender equality. In our modern world women are the legal and social equals of men, and, thanks to readily available birth control, they are rapidly becoming the sexual equals too. A new and improved Christianity will have to recognize these facts and will therefore have to treat women as being as fully human as men.

A new and improved Christianity will have to recognize that a code of sexual morality that demanded premarital abstention from sexual love makes no sense. Once upon a time boys and girls got married in their late teens. Now typical young persons do not get married until well into their twenties. It is unrealistic to expect them to deprive themselves of sexual love until that late date. Christianity, if it is to remain relevant in the modern world, will have to adjust to the facts of the modern world.

Again, Christianity used to take it for granted that marriage was a lifelong thing. While lifelong monogamy may be an ideal, it is no longer a *practical* ideal for great numbers of persons. In the modern world many marriages break up, and the people who get divorced often marry new partners. While this is often a sad event for the couple in question, it is a common fact in modern life, and the church, instead counting this fact as a sin, must do its best to help such people through their transition.

Nowadays many older people whose marriage has come to an end either by death or by divorce, feel a need for sexual companionship while at the same time, for a variety of good reasons, do not wish to marry. The church, instead of denouncing such unions as sinful, must bless them.

Further, while the church, in its ignorance and prejudice, traditionally condemned homosexuality and homosexual relationships, today, thanks to the enlightenment provided by modern science and psychology, we know that gays and lesbians are born that way; and the church, instead of condemning these relationships, must bless them.

Spong suggests that the church, which has always blessed marriage, must devise ceremonies to bless premarital cohabitation, to bless divorce, to bless post-marital sexual relationships, and to bless homosexual relationships. Rather oddly, he makes no proposal to bless polygamous relationships; he seems to expect that couples involved in these nontraditional sexual relationships will be monogamous. Nor does he propose blessings for adulterous relationships. He believes that persons involved in these nontraditional relationships should be faithful to their partners; he does not suspect that a rejection of old-fashioned Christian sexual morality will encourage adultery.

As for passages in the Bible that condemn premarital, post-marital, and homosexual relationships, Spong explains them away. He says that if you read the Bible carefully and if you understand the social, economic, and historical circumstances in which these Biblical condemnations were formulated, you will see either (a) that these Biblical passages do not mean what we have traditionally thought they meant (for example, the great sin of Sodom, says Spong, was not sodomy; it was inhospitality), or (b) that Biblical condemnations do not apply today, in a world radically changed from the ancient world.

You may wonder why Spong, who rejects many old and great doctrines of Christianity and who rejects Christian sexual morality, calls himself a Christian. I wonder too. In fact he is not a Christian. Rather, he is a splendid example of how far liberal Protestantism will go in clinging to the name Christian while tossing overboard almost all the content of Christianity.

Fletcher and Spong were perhaps the most conspicuous of the liberal Protestant ministers who accepted the sexual revolution, but they were not the only ones. Far from it. They were only the most famous. Thousands of ministers, including countless seminary professors, have taught essentially the same lessons. Liberal Protestantism in the USA today, though it still thinks of itself a kind of Christianity, has largely done away with the old Christian idea that chastity is a great virtue and has largely done away with the idea of sexual sin. It has accepted the secular humanist (that is, atheistic) idea of sexual morality.

Now some liberal Protestant may complain that I am being unfair. "There is an important difference," he will say, "between our liberal Protestant idea of sexual freedom and the atheistic idea of the same. For the atheist, the idea is: 'almost anything goes.' Provided you and your partner consent to the sexual act, and provided you do not molest children, and provided you take precautions against disease and unwanted pregnancy—provided you take care of these three things, you are free (the atheist will say) to do whatever you like with whomever you like. But we liberal Christians add that the sexual act must be motivated by love, and by "love" we have in mind two things: (a) the relationship between the two partners must be based on mutual respect and, to some significant degree at least, on mutual affection; and (b) the two partners must intend that their sexual relationship be for one another's benefit, this "benefit" being something better than mere fun or pleasure."

I grant that. I grant that this is what many liberal Protestant ministers and writers and seminary professors have in mind when they give their blessing to sexual conduct that violates traditional or old-fashioned rules of Christian sexual morality. I even grant that the evil of sexual freedom is mitigated when practiced by couples who love one another in the sense of the word "love" noted in the immediately preceding paragraph. All the same, I say two things. First, that this liberal Protestant idea of sexual morality is an idea that is in radical contradiction to the sexual morality held not only by Jesus, Paul, John, Augustine but also the sexual morality held by Luther, Calvin, Zwingli, and ten thousand other teachers of Protestant sexual morality. It is a new morality dating from the second half of the twentieth century, having nothing to do with the sexual morality of Christianity's first 1,900 years. Second, by endorsing a "Christian" version of sexual freedom, liberal Protestant ministers are opening the door to the fully atheistic version. A Christianized version of sexual freedom is but an anteroom to the full version. In short, liberal Protestantism has been, and continues to be, a major contributor to the advance of the sexual revolution. And since the sexual revolution is a thing of atheistic provenance, liberal Protestantism is a major contributor to the advance of atheism in America. It is a halfway house, a stopping place along the highway, on the downhill journey from Christianity to full-fledged atheism.

EPILOGUE

Where Do We Go from Here?

I have presented three sexual revolutions. Here in this final chapter, I will offer some guesses as to the future of these three revolutions. And I say "guesses" because that is all they are. I have no crystal ball; I cannot see the future. I can do no more than offer my best guesses.

The Modern Sexual Revolution

Since the champions of the sexual revolution have shown no signs of bringing their revolution to a close, where will they go next? And after they have gone there, what will follow?

Will they advocate the legalization of polygamy? I think they will.

Will they advocate the moral acceptance of polyamory? Certainly.

Will they advocate the legalization of incest among consenting adults? Yes—but with the proviso that no children be born of these incestuous unions.

Will they advocate lowering the age of sexual consent? Very probably. It is either sixteen or eighteen in the fifty American states at the moment. To the sexual liberationist mind, it is unreasonable for a boy or girl to have to wait till such an advanced age to have legally permissible sex. And of course many boys and girls, perhaps even most of them, are not waiting. Is it not time for the law to catch up with reality?

Will they advocate legalization of prostitution (sex work, as they like to call it)? Yes. Indeed they already are advocating this.

Will they advocate public acceptance of pedophilia as a morally legitimate sexual orientation? (When I speak of "pedophilia" here I am speaking of a sexual interest in pre-pubescent children.) Yes, but they will make a distinction between two things. (a) A pedophiliac *orientation*, which, they will argue, some people are born with; and therefore such an orientation is totally blameless. (b) Pedophiliac *behavior* (that is, sexual contact with very young children). This, the champions of sexual liberation will argue, needs to be handled with care. It is morally permissible only when it is of positive value to the child. But can sexual relations between a young child and an adult ever be good for the child? It will not be difficult to find sexual liberationists who will argue that such relations can be, at least in certain circumstances, good for the child; nor will it be difficult to find certain leftist child psychologists who will agree with them.

Liberationists will usually (but not always) say that these sexual contacts should be approved ahead of time by at least one parent or guardian of the child. But will any parent give his or her approval to this kind of thing? Of course. Think of the parents, more than a few of them, who encourage their little kids to claim a transgender identity. Some parents will do anything to be thought really up-to-date. "Look at my little boy/girl. He/she is engaging in a mutually beneficial love relationship with a gentle and caring adult. Most parents, alas, are so narrow-minded that they would not allow such a thing, no matter how much it may benefit their child. Not me. I'm super-cool."

Will they advocate the legalization of bestiality (sex with animals)? Probably not. But given their principles, I do not see why they should not.

Will they advocate the legalization of necrophilia (sex with human corpses)? Probably not. But again, given their principles, I do not see why they should not.

The Protestant Sexual Revolution

American Protestantism, as I have said above, is divided into two camps: liberal (or modernistic) Protestantism and Evangelical (or old-fashioned) Protestantism. Liberal Protestantism has already rejected the sexual ethic of old-fashioned Protestantism, the ethic that met with the approval of Luther, Calvin, and the other leading figures of the Reformation. Instead liberal Protestantism has pretty much endorsed the sexual ethic of modern (atheistic or semi-atheistic) sexual liberationists; and in any case, it has offered it no resistance. I expect it will continue to do the same in the future. And so, as sexual liberationists become more and more radical, so will liberal Protestants. In the end I expect that liberal Protestantism will largely—though not entirely—fade away.

I say "not entirely" because there will always be more than a few people who will think of themselves as Christians even though they have dropped almost all of the Christian belief system. The liberal Protestant option will always be available as a halfway house—a motel on the highway so to speak—for former Christians (Catholics or Evangelicals) who are on the downhill road to agnosticism or atheism. And it will also be available as a halfway house for former atheists or agnostics who are traveling uphill toward old-fashioned Christianity. But for the most part liberal Protestantism will be distinguishable from atheism and agnosticism in name only, and the denominations controlled by liberal Protestants will either collapse or become frankly non-Christian.

This is what happened to Unitarianism. It began as a Christian denomination, but eventually became so liberal that it decided, quite honestly, that it was no longer Christian. But the denomination owned many old and often handsome church buildings. What was it to do with them? Well, today they serve as Sunday morning meeting places for nice people, most of them atheists or agnostics, who like to get together once a week to reinforce one another in their "progressive" moral and political beliefs. After a few edifying readings (some of them from the Bible), plus the unenthusiastic singing of an old hymn or two, plus a politically correct sermon/reflection from the minister, they adjourn and have coffee and cookies.

Something like that is what will happen, I suspect, to liberal Protestantism generally. Protestant denominations that were once mighty forces in American life will become mere shadows of their former selves. But they will still own many handsome church buildings, and they will not want them to go to waste. A number of things will happen to these venerable buildings. (a) Some of them will be sold and converted to restaurants. (b) Some of the smaller ones will be sold and converted into private homes or condos. (c) Some will be purchased by developers and torn down. (d) Some will be sold to conservative Protestants and re-purposed as Evangelical or Pentecostal churches. (e) Some will be sold to Muslims and re-purposed as mosques. (f) Some few will retain their denominational name and, like Unitarian churches, will be re-purposed as Sunday gathering places for ex-Christians who like to keep up their fine old habits of church-going and fellowship.

Evangelical Protestantism, I expect, will retain its allegiance to traditional Christian doctrine and to traditional Christian morality, including sexual morality. This is what they have managed to do for five hundred years—despite the temptations offered by the principle of private judgment, despite the "acids of modernity,"[1] despite the example offered by liberal Protestantism, and despite the tremendous growth of religious unbelief over the last century and more.

Of course the Evangelical world is not a static thing. It loses members all the time due to one or more of the factors itemized in the preceding paragraph. Its more modern-minded younger persons often drift away, either into liberal Protestantism or into outright unbelief. But at the same time it is constantly recruiting new members, people who find that they are radically dissatisfied with the culture of disbelief and moral permissiveness that pervades much of present-day America. Such people, when they realize that have a choice between a culture of atheism and "old-time religion," feel they have to choose the latter.

I should add that if American Catholicism becomes genuinely Catholic, many conservative Protestants will turn to the Catholic Church, either joining it or becoming its allies in a "war" against atheism and sexual license.

1 This useful phrase comes from Walter Lippmann's book, now nearly 100 years old, *A Preface to Morals.*

The Catholic Sexual Revolution

When the modern sexual revolution swept America in the 1960s and '70s, American Catholicism, it seems to me, missed a golden opportunity. Half of America went mad in its enthusiasm for sexual freedom, and many if not most Catholics, being good Americans, went along with this madness, or at least offered no significant opposition to it. But not all Americans went mad, and neither did all Catholics. From east to west and from north to south, scores of millions of Americans, both Catholic and non-Catholic, felt that this enthusiasm for sexual freedom was indeed something like madness, and a very dangerous madness at that. But these dissenters tended to be quiet. They were a silent majority—or if not quite a majority at least a very numerous minority. They realized that their pro-chastity leanings were very unfashionable. They realized that if they were to speak up they would be laughed at. And as time went by they realized that they would be not only ridiculed but also censured as anti-woman and anti-gay; that is, they would be condemned as sexist and homophobic, as bigots and haters. And so for the most part they held their peace.

The leaders of the Catholic Church in the USA (and by "leaders" I mean bishops and priests) could have spoken for these people who dissented from the sexual revolution, could have been their great representative—whether the dissenters were Catholics or non-Catholics. But for the most part Catholic priests and bishops did not—and this failure to speak out often and emphatically against sexual freedom is the missed "golden opportunity" mentioned above. Oh, there was of course no official repeal of the traditional Catholic bans on fornication, unmarried cohabitation, divorce, marital contraception, adultery, and homosexual practice. And to some notable extent the Church's leaders made it clear that the Church disapproved of abortion; but even with regard to abortion they did not make nearly as much noise as they might have.

Instead our leaders, with here and there some notable and noble exceptions (I am thinking for example of Fr. Frank Pavone), adopted an attitude of, "Let's not talk about this. Let us pretend we do not know what is happening."

By way of justification for their silence they said things like this to themselves.

- “Jesus promised that his Church will always survive.”
- “We survived the Reformation, the French Revolution, Communism, and Nazism, not to mention two World Wars. We will survive the sexual revolution too.”
- “If we speak about sex matters we will irritate ten parishioners for every one we edify.”
- “Everybody knows what the Church teaches about sexual morality. No need for me to bore them with reiteration.”
- “Annoyed parishioners will reduce their contributions, both monetary and otherwise, to the parish.”
- “If I keep harping on sex matters, rich Catholics whom I rely on to contribute to my diocesan charities will think that I am a trouble-making bishop.”
- “Some annoyed parishioners will write to the bishop telling him that I am being uncharitable; and the bishop will tell me to cool it.”
- “Young people will be so annoyed that they will abandon the faith.”
- “Gays and their relatives will be so annoyed that they will abandon the faith.”

It goes without saying that the emphasis on Catholic sexual values would have driven many people out of the Church, people more attuned to the values of American secularism than to the values of Jesus Christ and the religion he founded. But the vacancies caused by these losses would have been replenished, and more than replenished, by the millions of non-Catholics who would have streamed into the Church when they discovered that the Catholic Church was giving voice to their own feelings about the ongoing sexual revolution. “I am not alone in my doubts as to the merits of sexual freedom,” people would say. “I am not alone in my disgust. The ancient and honorable Roman Catholic Church agrees with me.”

It was a great piece of historical bad luck that the sexual revolution hit America at the same moment that the reforms associated with Vatican II were hitting the Catholic Church. Vatican

II—or perhaps I should say "the spirit of Vatican II"—was teaching Catholics, and especially the younger generation of priests, to be "open" to the secular world that lay beyond the boundaries of the Catholic ghetto.

And what was the secular world especially teaching during the 1960s and '70s? It was teaching lessons in freedom, including sexual freedom. While it was hard for Catholics to applaud sexual freedom, it was equally hard, and probably even more hard, for them to denounce it, so caught up were they in the "spirit" of Vatican II.

Somewhat like the division between liberal and conservative Protestants mentioned above, but to a lesser degree, there is a growing division between liberal and conservative Catholics. I expect that with time this division will grow wider, but that it will never grow as wide as the split between liberal and conservative Protestants. Liberal Protestants feel free to drop virtually all traditional Christian teachings; I cannot imagine that liberal Catholics will ever go nearly that far. They feel free to reject, or at least to *soften*, certain Catholic teachings on many sex-related matters. They do not feel that premarital sex is a sin; or if it is, then it must be a venial sin, not the mortal sin Catholicism has long imagined. They feel that marital contraception is not at all sinful—except in those few cases in which a couple uses contraception, not to exclude pregnancy on this or that occasion, but to keep a marriage permanently childless. They feel that homosexual conduct, which may well be sinful when carried on promiscuously, is morally acceptable when done with caution (to protect against disease) and affection by persons who are "born that way."

As for abortion, they agree with the Church that it is a very serious wrong. They feel, however, that the culpability of women having abortions is often greatly reduced because of their social and economic circumstances, and not infrequently reduced to zero; and in any case they feel that abortion should be permitted by the law. Further, they keep reminding themselves that there are many serious sins besides abortion; for instance, indifference to poverty and war and racism. They agreed with Pope Francis when he said that Catholics should not "obsess" about abortion.

But this softening on matters of sex is as far as Catholic liberals are usually willing to go explicitly. They are not willing to make a public issue regarding other articles of belief—even when they do not personally subscribe to these articles. For instance, many Catholic liberals do not honestly believe in the Virgin Birth, or the physical Resurrection of Jesus, or the Divinity of Jesus, or the Triune nature of God, or Hell, or the Real Presence of Christ in the Eucharist, or the infallibility of the pope. But they generally keep their skepticism on these matters to themselves, something they do not do when it comes to sex-related matters.

Catholics who grow more and more liberal with regard to Catholic dogmas generally, both sex-related and others, only rarely try to take the entire Church with them; for it is too absurd to imagine a Catholic Church without Catholic doctrines. If they are logical, as many of them will prove to be in the long run, they will simply drift away from the Church and join the ranks of secular humanists (*de facto* atheists). This will leave the Church in the USA in the hands of a relatively small group of true believers, true-believing laity guided by true-believing bishops and priests. This reversion to a Catholic Church that is truly Catholic will no doubt take many decades. But when and if it happens, the American Catholic Church, by that time a numerically small thing, will be in a position to rebuild; and in its rebuilding it will be able to draw to itself, either as full-fledged members or as Protestant fellow-travelers, that large minority of the American people who, even many decades from now, will have no stomach for atheism or its ethic of sexual license.

I suspect that fifty or one hundred years from now, the USA will be divided, with regard to religion, into three main groups: (1) secular humanists (that is to say, atheistic humanists) and their fellow travelers (liberal Christians and liberal Jews); (2) Evangelical Protestants and their fellow travelers (Mormons); and (3) orthodox Catholics and their fellow travelers (Eastern Orthodox Christians, Orthodox Jews).

My guess (and it is little more than a guess) is that the #1 group will be numerically the largest, and that its size and its consequent social and cultural power will drive Evangelicals and orthodox Catholics into one another's arms. When I speak of this last development, I do not mean that Evangelicals and Catholics will merge. They will not do that, for their old doctrinal disagreements will not allow such a development. But their doctrinal disagreements, which loomed large when the USA was an almost thoroughly Christian nation, will seem minor in a nation that is dominated by an atheistic worldview. Besides, they agree on almost all the main Christian doctrines—those summed up in the Nicene Creed. And they are in agreement in their opposition to the sexual revolution. And so, while there will be no merger of the two, it is likely that there will be a practical alliance between the two in the cultural and political struggle against atheism.

Alas, I will not live long enough to see whether my predictions prove to be true. But save this book. Give it to your grandchildren and let them give a grade to my predictions.

CPSIA information can be obtained
at www.ICGtesting.com
Printed in the USA
BVHW041012080322
630895BV00009B/169

9 781943 901210